EVEN MORE KETCHUP
THAN SALSA:
THE FINAL DOLLOP

JOE CAWLEY

EVEN MORE KETCHUP THAN SALSA
THE FINAL DOLLOP

The making of this book was supported by many, many kind and generous people, not least of which were my Mum, Carole Cawley-Smith, and my sister, Yvonne Smith, both of whom are now bestowed with the grand title of 'Ketchup Angels'.
Heartfelt thanks to you both.
X X

PART ONE

EVEN MORE KETCHUP THAN SALSA

Chapter One

If the first six months of running the Smugglers Tavern had been a baptism of fire, the subsequent years were about as much fun as bobbing for apples in a vat of acid.

Yes, we'd thwarted the multi-pronged attack posed by Tenerife's bungling and bewildered expats and holidaymakers, but what we didn't realise was that our enemies were regrouping. Not only that, but those enemies had made camp a lot closer to home. It was now a sleeper cell, several sleeper cells in fact. Enemies within that would soon pounce and make our encounters with exploding gas bottles, Czechoslovakian squatters and big-time Charlies seem like chapters from Enid Blyton.

Our life-flip seemed so long ago now. 26,188 hours and 15 minutes to be exact. We'd been running the Smugglers Tavern for less than three years, yet it seemed a lifetime since Joy, David, Faith and I had arrived at Reina Sofia Airport ashen-faced and clutching the remnants of our pre-Tenerife lives in an assortment of plastic shopping bags and borrowed suitcases.

A lot had happened since June 1991. For a start, we'd lost Faith – David's wife, that is, not the spiritual will to carry on. It took her just three months to realise bar life wasn't for her.

The landscape had changed too. El Beril, the holiday complex where we lived and worked, had entered puberty. A beach had developed in its nether regions, a mass of golden sand covering what had previously been a stubble of craggy rocks.

The sand had been vacuumed up from the seabed with the help of finances pooled from a tag-team of Tenerife tourism authorities, the local Adeje council and developers of the Altamira Aparthotel across the car park from the Smugglers.

The new beach boosted our fortunes with a stream of parched beach-goers who bravely slogged up Cardiac Hill in desperate search of rehydration. Perversely, this proved a mixed blessing: with business now so brisk, the Smugglers claimed our every waking hour, leaving David, Joy and me with little chance to experience the refreshing waters, jamboree of colours and sybaritic sunbathing for ourselves. Our new beach was little more than tantalising eye candy that teased and toyed with us.

Greenery had sprouted right across the half-square-mile of our complex. Great necklaces of purple bougainvillea draped over the pine-framed bungalow windows like Hawaiian garlands, at sunset the silhouettes of palm trees now stretched up and along the whitewashed walls of second-floor apartments, and giant thumbs of lime-green cacti poked from black volcanic cinders in the waist-high bedding boxes that lined the walkways.

Although the number of bungalows and one- and two-storey apartments had doubled in the three years we'd been there – to around 200 units, arranged in gentle, ochre-roofed tiers between the beach and the main road to La Caleta – the monumental backdrop was still prevalent. The volcanic peak of Mount Teide was still visible over the serrated ridge of the Adeje massif, its plunging slopes levelling off below the old town of Adeje, then again through the village of Fañabe, before softening to a barely noticeable gradient thick with banana plantations that spilled pools of green onto the dusty land between the TF-1 motorway and El Beril.

Initially we had enjoyed splendid isolation from the bawdiness of Playa de las Américas, the main resort three headlands and a rocky stomp away. Now civilisation was creeping towards us as property developers fought over every inch of the 3 miles of prime coastline between El Beril and downtown. Hotels were popping up faster than teenage acne and, in the remaining spaces where concrete wasn't yet clawing at the sky, white chalk lines like those at a crime scene outlined plots as they were picked off by sharpshooters from foreign hotel groups.

The immediate scenery around the squat commercial centre that housed the Smugglers Tavern had also changed. Whereas before we had held court among a captive audience of mostly British holidaymakers and residents, in January 1994 culinary competition arrived in the form of Chez Claude. This high-class French restaurant occupied one of the small retail units on the level above us, reached via a short walkway over our terrace. It was owned and staffed by a French family from Paris, whose collective noses defied all laws of gravity, permanently reaching for the heavens in disdain at having to walk the same earth as lowlifes like us.

Monsieur Claude was remarkable not just for his internationally famed cuisine, but also for an exceptionally poor toupee that capped his rotund form with an errant clump of black. For someone so esteemed in the Paris catering world, it was surprising to see such a poorly presented topping. Either the wig didn't have a front or back label or it had the ability to revolve randomly, as it seemed to face a different way each time we saw him. One day a straggle of low fringe would shade his eyes; the following day that straggle would be tickling the back of his neck while his forehead would be naked save for a high-floating tuft.

On one of the rare occasions when our interaction extended beyond complete indifference, I learnt that Monsieur Claude had been a top chef in Paris for many years, until his heart had decided to work flexi-time and he had been forced to retire. But with garlic in his veins, it wasn't long before the lure of the ladle had enticed him back to catering and in an act of compromise with his wife, Margaux, they uprooted to open a restaurant in less of a pressure-cooker environment. I would have found out more but at that point Margaux returned, clomping into the kitchen and eyeing me as if I was something Claude had brought in on the sole of his shoe.

Not only did this new restaurant attract a raft of higher-class diners from other parts of the island, it also upped the ante in terms of the quality of cuisine in El Beril. With plates of *confit de canard* and *escargots* gracing the starched linen upstairs, downstairs in the Smugglers Tavern, we felt compelled to raise our game too. We made extra efforts to ensure that the burger buns weren't stale, minimal egg shell found its way into the omelettes, and salads were delivered to tables relatively pest-free.

Competition on the drinking front consisted of

two venues, the first situated immediately above the Smugglers Tavern four doors along from Chez Claude on the upper level of our mini, two-storey commercial centre. The main source of revenue for the cubbyhole Bar Arancha was vodka – ceaseless rounds of shots consumed by resident timeshare reps who snuck to the bar in-between bouts spent extorting money from the naive and fleece-able.

It was manned from morning till night by Ernesto. Perma-stubble, protruding belly, bloodshot eyes and a constant frown belied his thirty-something years and suggested that life had not gone exactly according to plan. When he wasn't borrowing vodka from us to keep up with the timeshare reps' thirst, he was serving drinks, cleaning the windows or plying the local constabulary with free beer in a spirited bid to avoid paying the fines he accrued as a result of having no legal right whatsoever to ply his wares.

Ernesto may have been an ugly mess of strife and stress but his wife Marie was quite the opposite; she was the epitome of Andalusian attractiveness. Her huge almond-shaped eyes peeked seductively through a fringe of black sheen and her tanned cleavage of canyonesque proportions drew admirers from afar. In fact, if Ernesto had decided to comply with the authorities' repeated requests that he cease trading, the occupancy of Bar Arancha would still be just as high so long as Marie plonked herself on a stool in the middle of the bar and did nothing at all but paint her nails. Which is just as well as no matter what time you popped your head in to ask for your bottle of vodka back you'd find Marie plonked on a stool in the middle of the bar doing nothing at all but painting her nails.

Mikey and Alli, their two sons of nine and five, were also often on hand to make up the numbers. Mikey's main role was to keep Alli out of mischief. Alli, often dressed in nothing but ill-fitting underpants, had decided that the best way to support the family business was to spend his time cheerily showering our patrons with leaves pulled from an overhanging bedding box; or stones, when the plants had been plucked bare; or on one particularly memorable occasion, the actual bedding box itself.

It became part of our daily routine to trot upstairs and inform Ernesto that we'd prefer it if his youngest offspring refrained from hurling lethal objects at our customers. Ernesto would roll his eyes, apologise profusely and make great show of first slapping Alli about the head for his misdemeanours, then berating poor Mikey for not having foiled his little brother's attempts at murdering the British population of El Beril.

Mikey devised his own punishment for his little brother, a custodial sentence which entailed locking him in the *basura* 'bunker' next to the El Beril shops and bars, where the community dumped its rubbish. Alli's frightened cries and little fists banging on the inside of the corrugated metal doors always made for a curtailed imprisonment as either we, or one of the other business owners would race to his rescue. Meanwhile Marie would smile sweetly from her pedestal, blowing on her nails, blissfully dismissive of any near-fatal devilment.

The other venue that competed for our trade was the Altamira hotel bar, a soulless rectangle of whitewashed walls, cheap cane furniture and limp potted plants on Floor 1 of the six-storey aparthotel. By day, sliding glass doors behind the bar area were folded back, inviting swimming-pool users to leave a slippery trail of water on the polished marble floor. This startled the daily parade of senior citizens, who found the sudden increase in velocity a poor match for their impaired mobility.

Fortunately for us, those trusted with the management of the Altamira bar had more humour than hospitality skills, judging by the succession of clowns employed. Although neatly suited in the standard Spanish bar uniform of white short-sleeved shirt and black trousers, all other elements necessary to providing hotel guests with an amiable refreshment service were lacking. Enthusiasm, efficiency and politeness were notable by their absence. In their place were disgruntlement, slovenliness and a rudeness that teetered on the brink of assault. Ask for half a Dorada – if indeed you could find one of the bar staff – and the best you could hope for was a flat beer served with striking indifference in a lipstick-smeared glass. If your order required them to do anything more challenging than pour a beer or pop a bottle top – make a coffee, for instance – you might as well have spat in their eye and blasphemed their children, such was the reaction.

Needless to say, the hotel bar didn't attract too many loyal patrons, even on weekend nights. The lure of third-rate flamenco and a 'Fun' Disco Nite that clearly wasn't, did little to compensate for the sterile environment and reluctant bar staff.

With competition encouragingly inadequate, we

were the outright winner when it came to sheer volume of customers, but were any other decent bars to arrive on the scene, they could potentially damage our bottom line. We prayed that they would never come, and our prayers were answered. At least for a while.

There seemed to be a common theme in the set-up and running of both Chez Claude and Bar Arancha in that the burden shouldered by the marital partners was askew. I suppose with most 'family-run' bars and restaurants, the instigating partner speeds full ahead in a spray of blind enthusiasm while the other is dragged along spluttering through a turbulent wake of doubt and resentment. This had certainly happened in my case, initially. In the Ram's Head on that rainy day in Bolton back in 1991, Joy had steamrollered me into submission with pints of Extra Strong and a volley of persuasive talk about buying a bar in Tenerife. 'Go back and work behind that crappy stall and stink of fish for the rest of our lives, then,' she'd countered when my reticence, caution and doubts surfaced.

She'd had a point, of course. But going into partnership with my brother and his wife, taking on a debt of £165,000 for a business we had zero experience of, on an island whose language we couldn't speak, still seemed a bit of an extreme response, when we could simply have gone out and bought some extra bars of Imperial Leather instead.

In such situations there's bound to be one party always banging the drum a little louder than the other. In our position, in case you haven't gathered, it was Joy who threw caution to the wind, and me who subsequently raced around like a lunatic manically trying to collect it all up again.

Unbeknown to me, another inequality had surfaced in our own business. While I was happy to hide in the kitchen, at the beck and call of the order board stuck to the fridge door, Joy was at the beck and call of the hundreds of customers who passed through our doors on a daily basis. Each one of them expected jovial and personal attention non-stop, regardless of how Joy was feeling that day, how little sleep she'd had the night before and whatever personal turmoil was battling for attention in her head. In fact Joy could have turned up for work with blood spurting from a severed artery in her neck and customers would still have stood there blinking, wanting to indulge in a little light-hearted banter.

While I had become a slave to the order board, she had become a slave to each and every one of our patrons, in the spotlight 24/7 – or at least 14/7. She was proud of her popularity but all too aware she had to dance to their tune to keep the till ringing and to retain her crown as 'Queen of Tenerife pubs'.

My complete ignorance of the pressure she was under and the tight corner that our customers and Joy herself had pinned her in, had created a smouldering volcano that was shortly to erupt. The mask that she wore, ever-stiffening, ever-squeezing, suffocating her own personality, was near breaking point.

I just didn't see it coming.

JOE CAWLEY

CHAPTER TWO

As lunchtimes went, this one had been incredibly slow. An unusually hot May breeze rolled through the open double doors of the Smugglers Tavern, bringing the scent of coconut oil from bikini-clad holidaymakers and stirring it with the smell of musty beer from the bar and the aroma of roast chicken from the kitchen.

When Joy had first proposed buying a bar on a sub-tropical island, and after I'd got over the initial shock, my visions had been of a small bar dressed in Mediterranean blues, with an outlook across a beach bordered with palm trees and orchids, white speedboats carving frothy lines in a sparkling sea, and exotic islands rising in the near distance.

In reality, our outlook was a flaking, whitewashed wall 15 feet away at the far end of our terrace, rising 10 feet to the car park above. Its only interesting feature was a corrugated metal door where the electricity meter was hidden and from where cockroaches would sprint to the first drops of spilt beer and food.

As the bar was below ground level, nestling in what was more or less a terraced trench between the edge of the El Beril complex and the hotel car park, our only visual contact with civilisation was via those who chose to descend into our commercial world. This world comprised a cluster of units, known as *locales*, most of which were still vacant. The Smugglers Tavern occupied two *locales* and was flanked by an empty unit to either side. Next but one to our left was Patricia's British supermarket, the only other place currently open for business on our subterranean level. Above and to the left of Patricia's was a footbridge that provided access to the *locales* at ground level and cast the terrace of the (also still empty) corner *local* beneath it in permanent shade.

The rest of us got plenty of sun on our tiled terraces. In fact, the daily supply of rays was mentioned almost every time something went wrong, which was often. 'Well, at least it's sunny!' all the expats would say, as if this was the antidote to each and every calamity.

Today was no exception. Sunlight sliced through the plate-glass frontage, cutting the bar in two. A neat line slowly advanced along the ochre floor tiles towards the kitchen doorway and bathroom corridor in the back wall, engulfing all that it met in midday sun. It climbed the dark, round, wooden legs of our two rows of tables, paled the salmon tablecloths and leapt from smeared glass tops onto the white walls and wood-beamed ceiling; in its wake, it illuminated handprints and smudges above the tall backs of the wall benches that were padded in fading patterns of amber and lemon paisley.

Joy and I sat directly opposite the bench seats, perched on waist-high wooden stools with elbows resting on the black-painted bar top. Behind us, a kaleidoscope of colours danced from sunlit spirits gathering dust on the lowest of the mirrored, floor-to-ceiling bottle shelves.

We gawped absent-mindedly at our only two customers. The two senior citizens grazed on plates of beans on toast, slurped two mugs of PG Tips, then sat back contentedly, hands clasped on laps, without a single word offered to each other.

The man wore a purple Hawaiian shirt and sailor's cap, belying his attitude of complete dejection. Shoulders, mouth and jowls all pointed to the floor, where two spindly white legs sprouted from slate-grey socks and beige sandals.

Slumped next to him was a lady of somewhat larger proportions. Pallid layers of flab spilled over the elasticated waistband of ill-fitting crinoline shorts whose puce floral pattern was strangely reminiscent of the shower curtains from my 1970s childhood home.

It was a scene I'd seen many times before, both as bar owner and as customer, and one tinged with sadness. Two people, presumably once in love, now sharing a life together but treating each other like an extra layer of clothing in winter – a comfortable and practical union but hardly worthy of conversation.

Back in the early years of my relationship with Joy, when childhood friendship finally slipped into late-teen romance and the sharing of intimate secrets became an obsession, it was impossible to imagine that Joy and I might also reach that point in our journey when topics had been exhausted and the flame of interest in each other was barely a flicker. But, quite frankly, the bar and its patrons had become the mistress, constantly demanding time and attention that previously we'd spent on each other. And now, even though free time was rare, we dreaded the quiet periods, when the spotlight of silence illuminated just how far apart we'd grown.

This was one of those times. I felt we should be talking, but in truth we had nothing to say to each other. We worked in the same environment, heard the same stories from customers, then went home and longed for nothing but sleep to ease the exhaustion and ready ourselves for the next Groundhog Day.

As it was, the lady broke the silence as she tried to stifle a burp with the back of her hand but only succeeded in expelling a second burst of gas out of her rear. Either immune to his wife's flatulence or completely indifferent, her husband didn't stir. Her eyes flicked sideways to see if we'd noticed the twin gun salute. We stared back, equally unmoved.

A solitary fly buzzed over our heads, first landing in my hair, then Joy's. Neither of us bothered to shoo it away. The overhead fans rotated slowly, almost begrudgingly, stirring the stifling air but not cooling it. The hands on the large railway station clock above the open door inched towards two in the afternoon, the time when my brother, David would relieve us of our shift.

I trudged with flip-flops flapping on terracotta tiles back to the kitchen to continue the daily ritual of preparing for the evening rush, stepping through the open doorway into a wall of 140-degree heat.

There is much to be said for having an 'open' kitchen in a bar or restaurant – if you're a customer. At least you can see if the chef has some unsociable malady that causes him or her to violently sneeze or vomit onto your eagerly awaited feast, or check if he or she harbours any open wounds that threaten to seep pus into your *soup du jour*. Before committing to the waiter you can also do a quick scan to make sure that the kitchen isn't overrun with cockroaches, flies or other ugly critters that

14

will take delight in scampering over your plate, or worse still, lurk under lettuce leaves only to be discovered during a sickening crunch on what you anticipated would be lump-free gastronomy.

Most of the downsides apply only if you're the chef in said open kitchen. Apart from trying to hide all of the aforementioned, you're also at the mercy of any well-intentioned customer who decides to wander in and engage you in friendly but immensely boring banter, as some of our more regular patrons were wont to do.

Although there was still a lot to learn, like how to change a barrel of beer without potentially blowing my head off, I *had* mastered the art of entering a state of glazed serenity when listening to the endless ramblings of our more personality-challenged customers. Some people just do not know when to shut up. I mean what possible pleasure do they think could be squeezed out of a one-way conversation on the dubious talents of a patron's pet? But still the tale would go on and on, as if my whole purpose in life was to act as cannon fodder for personal boasts while trying to cook eleventeen breakfasts and a baked-bean omelette.

Thankfully, today I was alone, for now at least. I held the chest freezer lid wide open and rummaged deep into the icy depths, enjoying the blast of cold air. From below a brood of frozen chickens I plucked out a full tuna. In its natural environment this 24-inch specimen would have been a glory to behold, eyes bright and alert, its cobalt-blue body flashing through the water, free to roam the vast ocean wherever the current took it. Even when it was brought into the Smugglers on a length of fishing line – by Mario, the retired ex-owner of the bar, who was making a rare appearance in his former home territory – the sleek magnificence of the fish had caused heads to turn, jaws to drop. But three weeks in the chest freezer had done it no favours. Blue had become grey and the bright eyes were now cloudy and lifeless.

I thought back to the stall in Bolton market that Joy and I had left behind, to our daily routine of waking up at 3.30 with nothing to look forward to other than the stench of fish and a stream of tiring banter. Here in El Beril it was almost 2pm. Two thousand miles away, ruddy-faced Pat and his stall workers would be packing away the boxes of deadly tandoori chicken thighs, smoked mackerel and skinned rabbits. Hoses would be blasting bits of chicken skin and fish innards off the metal stalls onto the concrete floor and herding all the rubbish into damp piles in the middle of the deserted walkways. Darren and his snorkel jacket would be getting their daily dousing as he sloshed between stalls on a final cadge for copper coins, sweets and leftovers from other vendors. I wondered if, three years on, anybody else had escaped, and if so, had they found freedom and happiness?

I held the tuna up. Beads of sweat rolled off my elbow onto the boxes of hamburgers, chicken fillets and English sausages. I lowered the fish to eye level and felt a spike of sympathy. Just another piece of flesh waiting to be gorged on during the Smugglers' Special Friday Fish Night, washed down with an earthenware carafe of the finest carton red that the equivalent of 20p could buy.

My 'freedom' also felt like it had been frozen in a

perpetual state of monotony. Same thing every day: feed the masses, smile like an idiot, then clean, sleep, rinse and repeat.

While I philosophised with the dead fish, Joy sat picking her nails. Whereas before we would happily idle away this downtime, making each other laugh or challenging each other to perform daring stunts like working in the kitchen wearing nothing but an apron and a smile, now the periods of boredom were spent in silence.

It had recently dawned on me that Joy and I had become little more than work colleagues. Romance had long since been hounded out of town by the demands of needy patrons, daily chores and the energy-sapping summer heat.

'Have you taken the tuna out for tomorrow?' shouted Joy from the bar.

'Just doing it,' I mumbled. 'You put the boards out?'

'Yep.'

I took my apron off and went to pour myself a Coke from behind the bar, flicking a cockroach off the spill tray before I sat down with Joy again. Our only customers had departed.

'Want one?'

'Nah.'

'It's quiet.'

'Yeah.'

In the corner on one of the cushioned benches, Buster, the dog-attacking bar cat that had adopted us in our early months, briefly stirred. Unfurling from ginger ball, he stretched all four legs, looked at us both, yawned and went back to sleep. It was a fair statement of how our lives, and our

17

relationship, had become. Boring.

I idly watched a couple of flies copulate on a slice of freshly cut lemons... and then from out of the shadow of calm stepped chaos.

'What the jiddy!' said Joy.

In the doorway stood a familiar figure, carrying a guitar case and an inane grin.

It was Steve, the singer in the band I had played with back in England and in Boston, USA. Judging by his unsteady gait and wayward focus he'd already been drinking heavily.

'Band on tour!' he shouted, almost knocking me to the floor in a drunken embrace.

'What the bleedin' hell are you doing over here?' I asked.

'You invited us, you git. Don't you remember?' said Steve.

I looked at Joy. 'That was over three years ago! Thought you might give us a bit of warning or something,' I said.

'It wasn't only you. Met a guy on holiday in Stockport and got asked to join a band over here, so here I am. Just arrived, so I thought I'd look you up first, get a free beer and all that, eh?'

Joy went to pour him a half.

'Where are you staying then?' she said over her shoulder.

Steve patted the pockets of his black jeans then pulled a crumpled note from the pocket of his black shirt. 'O-r-o Neg-ro, wherever the hell that is. With a guy called Anthony, the bloke I met in Stockport. He's got a band here but the singer did one. I was just dicking around in England so thought I might as well. Plus, it means I get to see me old buddies again. How about it, Joyklet?'

Steve had coined her nickname during the band days. More than once she'd voiced her opinion about how vain and conceited he was, but there was no denying that he was a good-looking bastard with a raffish charm.

'Yeah, great.' Joy's mouth smiled sarcastically but her eyes had come to life, pleased to see a familiar face from outside our bar world.

'Why don't you stay with us for a while?' I suggested. 'Let Anthony know you're here then hook up with him later.'

'As long as Joyklet doesn't mind.' He stood with one arm draped round her shoulders. Even though he was half-cut and had just travelled 2,000 miles, Steve's short blonde coif was still immaculate, no doubt cemented into an Elvis quiff with half a can of Bristows extra-strong hairspray as usual.

'Err... I guess not. Just for a while. We can sort something out. Joe'll walk you to our apartment. I'll see you back there in a bit.'

~

At the apartment, Steve was in no mood to come down from his alcoholic euphoria and insisted we had a celebratory drink. Unfortunately, this turned into *several* beers, then whiskies and finally tequila on the terrace. Joy had come back and decided a siesta was preferable to a daytime session seeing as we were both due back on for a six o'clock shift in the bar. Rather than wake her, we opted to continue drinking in Bar Arancha, where I had to apologise to the owner, Ernesto, who understandably took an immediate dislike to Steve due to his excessive and very drunken flirting with his wife, Marie.

At ten past six I finally managed to stagger down to the Smugglers. Joy was on her own trying to cook two half chicken and chips for a couple of early diners. Another couple were waiting to be served at the bar.

'Sorry 'bout that,' I slurred, putting on my apron.

Joy slapped the tongs into my hand. 'Chips are nearly done.'

Half an hour later Steve stumbled back into the Smugglers and tried to hold a conversation with Joy as she flew round the restaurant taking and delivering orders.

As is the way with alcohol, the more he consumed, the higher the volume and bawdiness of his banter became, until Joy had to bribe him to return to the apartment with a bottle of house wine. From the kitchen I watched him stagger out, envious of his freedom and anxious as to the state of our home when Joy and I returned.

~

It wasn't one of my best ideas, to invite my former band to move to Tenerife. In fact, in hindsight it was quite possibly the single most disastrous decision I ever took. But it seemed like the right thing to do at the time – 'the time' being a hazy blur immediately after having consumed my fifth pint of Stella Artois at The Bakers Vaults in Stockport during the last gig I saw Steve and co play before I left for our new life in Tenerife.

I was in one of those jolly, foot-tapping moods

when the whole world seemed perfect and everyone was my friend. In short, I was pissed.

'You're brilliant, brilliant. Come to Tenerife, eh? You can play at our bar. Be brilliant, brilliant. Eh? Whadyasay?'

And the band, being in their usual state of post-gig dissipation, slurred their agreement without a second's thought.

When it actually came down to it, only Steve – the lead singer and bass player – had decided to go for it. Dominic, the guitarist in the three-piece, was engaged to Debbie, who possessed the ass of an angel and a pout that could paralyse at 40 feet. Unfortunately she also possessed the authority of a dictator and had absolutely no intention of giving up a steady job at a local accountant's for the sake of a band that was going nowhere fast. And so it was that sweet love snuffed out yet another rock and roll dream.

Jimmy, who had taken over my role as drummer when I left, also got cold feet, or rather realised that although the town of Romiley was about as appealing as a pig in a blender, it was *his* world and one that he couldn't persuade his mind or his heart to leave.

Unlike for Jimmy and Dominic, life on the dole while waiting for stardom held no appeal for Steve. Didn't need to. The son of an actor turned highly successful businessman, he was under a great deal of self-imposed pressure to 'prove his worth' just as his father had. He was a talented songwriter, played every instrument under the sun and had the looks of a young Sting before tantra took hold and decapitated his coolness. With the presence of a film star, a rich family and musical talent by the bucketful, I hated him. Actually, I didn't. I admired him greatly and he became a very good friend.

Naturally he had no shortage of female admirers, but he could never sustain an amorous partnership beyond a few weeks. Those of a more envious nature would say he was a spoilt rich kid with an ego that acted as an unwanted third party in a relationship. However, those that knew him better were aware that his major problem lay just below the belt buckle, a belt that would have been better if it had remained buckled more often.

Still, the pain of being dumped repeatedly inspired many self-penned melodies about social injustice and personal hardship that, were it not for the fact that he lived in a mansion and drove a Mercedes, would have been very easy to sympathise with. Poetic licence, I think it's called.

~

As it was, Steve had passed out pretty quickly once he'd returned to our apartment, judging by the amount of wine still left in the bottle. He lay comatose on the two-seater settee, long legs dangling over the end. Joy threw a blanket over him while I poured the remaining wine down the kitchen sink. We turned the lights out, climbed into bed, turned to face opposite walls, mumbled 'na-night' and were asleep in seconds as normal. Sleep was sacrosanct. Those six hours we had until we needed to be up again were precious and nothing could get in the way, not reading, romance nor any other interaction typical of a normal couple's relationship. Sleep ruled, full stop.

CHAPTER THREE

Steve's stay with Joy and me turned out to be a lot longer than the 'few days' we had initially offered. He made contact with Anthony and spent the odd night at his apartment, getting drunk and practising with the band, but had seemingly made no effort to find alternative accommodation, reserving his most frequent bouts of inebriation for chez Cawley.

Neither of us minded though. It gave us the chance to revisit the days of carefree rock and roll rebellion on those rare nights when we managed to find staff trustworthy enough not to burn the bar down, steal all the takings or get more drunk than the customers. For Joy it was simply a welcome distraction from repetitive routines and familiar faces. It was also a happy connection with the old, untroubled world that we had left behind.

Steve became a confidant for Joy, a pair of ears outside the bubble in which we lived. His arrival also resurrected a close buddy relationship for me; something else that the Smugglers had stolen from all of us – time for friends. He would offer advice, lend a hand and calm me down in the kitchen when my angry mutterings started to spill over into wild chastising over every petty request: 'extra tomato on the salad', I would repeat with a grimace; 'no mushrooms in the chicken in wine'; and, my special bugbear, 'no cheese on the cheeseburger' – 'duh... ask for a beefburger then!'

It wasn't until late in the summer of 94 though, when the band were gigging three to four nights a week, that Steve was in a position to finally move out and start paying rent. Knowing that he was used to his luxuries, I asked my mum if he could have her apartment for a while. She liked Steve and knew him from my band days so agreed readily, providing he moved out temporarily whenever she and my stepfather visited.

The second-floor apartment had the best position in the El Beril complex; it was bright and open-plan, with wooden balconies on three sides, overlooking the Atlantic Ocean 50 yards away, Cardiac Hill to the right and the soaring Adeje mountains in the distance behind. It befitted Steve's privileged upbringing and he was mighty pleased to have the whole apartment to himself, especially for the token rent that my mum had requested.

Happily settled, he'd taken to strolling down to the bar early on to share a coffee; he'd fill us both in on any gossip from back home and then help Joy prep in the kitchen ready for the day's onslaught while I did the daily cash-and-carry run. He became an extra pair of hands for us, and for David and whoever was assisting him at the time. Since David's wife Faith had returned to the UK two and a half years earlier, he had been partnered at work with a succession of short-term 'help', some of whom actually did help, and others who most certainly didn't.

The quality of these employees was extremely varied. 'Short-term help' is generally taken to mean a person or pool of people that you can call on as and when needed. Our staff seemed to think that 'help' meant 'help yourself', as in 'help yourself to drinks' or 'help yourself to cash from the till'. Most didn't seem to understand that because we gave them money we expected a little work in return. They considered this optional and preferred to just sit at the bar having a drink with customers, sunbathe on the terrace or catch forty winks stretched out on the chest freezer in the kitchen.

At the top of our employment tree when it came to quality was our longest-serving part-time helper, Robin, whose illustrious career at the Smugglers had begun almost three years earlier when she had just turned fourteen. Supermarket Patricia's pretty blonde daughter boasted an O level in flirting and an ability to hold her drink that belied her current age (seventeen) – a future landlady, if ever there was one.

At the less celebrated end of the range sat David's latest protégé, Sammy, who had recently arrived in El Beril from the Midlands, via the Veronicas nightlife strip. This quarter-mile block of iniquity on the seafront in Playa de las Américas was the most notorious club zone on the island, a magnet for dance-, drink- and drugs aficionados. Strobe-lit nightclubs competed in a decibel war on the two floors above ground, while the basements housed 'spillover' bars that kept the party going from 3am until breakfast for those with a surfeit of youthful, or chemically inspired, energy.

During the summer months, when schools and colleges were on holiday, the grassy bank in front of Veronicas would be packed with junior hedonists forcing down excessive amounts of alcohol, speed and ecstasy in great shows of bravado. Late-night traffic would be halted by masses of revellers spilling out of the clubs, beat-weary, big-eyed and bewildered.

Occasionally you'd notice the shutters of bars and clubs quickly descending in unison, a sure warning that trouble was imminent. Within seconds the dense carpet of youngsters would tear open as troops of heavy-handed policemen appeared from nowhere and waded in with batons flying to try and disperse the swarm.

While Sammy was working behind the bar in one of Veronicas' bigger clubs, her waist-length blonde hair, long, dramatic eyelashes, bulging cleavage and bum-hugging jeans had caught the attention of an Argentinean entrepreneur who immediately pledged his undying love and a personal platinum credit card. The former, Sammy could live without, but the latter had left her putty in his hands, even though he spent most of his time in South America. He immediately insisted she leave her job and proceeded to 'hide' her far from ogling eyes in his apartment in the Altamira hotel opposite the Smugglers. No sooner had she moved in, than the credit card was mysteriously blocked, presumably so Sammy didn't have the means to beggar off in a hurry.

Short on cash but banned from working downtown, she used her charm and looks to wheedle her way into David's good books, and he, unsurprisingly, was more than happy to have her work alongside him for a bit of spare cash. However, what she added in aesthetics she lost in profit. So familiar was she with the art of not paying her way, she thought nothing of letting others walk away without paying either. Needless to say, she was extremely popular with our customers. At regular intervals we'd pull her up about not charging customers, but it was difficult to be harsh.

'Sammy, did that couple pay anything for those drinks?'

'Aww, how can you make them pay? They've been telling me what a hard time they've been having this year... They're really lovely people. Don't be mean,' she'd reply and then go on to pout apologies in a singsong Midlands accent.

Sammy was like a bottle of top-shelf champagne: bubbly and fun to be around, but expensive to keep and a pain if consumed in large quantities. It didn't take long for Steve to fathom that out, and thanks to regular funds sent from his dad in England, he was the only one able to keep up with Sammy's insatiable appetite for the better things in life. He and Sammy would chat for ages, completely ignoring customers but sharing a laugh – and Steve's traveller's cheques. It was never admitted but was assumed all round that the two had become bed buddies, often heading downtown together and not reappearing until late in the morning.

Steve kept quiet, but I could tell from the over-exaggerated look of innocence when questioned that his belt had been unbuckled yet again. Unfortunately, so too could Sammy's Argentinean sugar daddy, who had returned unexpectedly late one night to find his apartment a) empty, b) a mess, and c) sporting a guitar case that clearly wasn't Sammy's.

It didn't take him long to discover who it belonged to. At eight the following morning while he was having breakfast, the apartment door flew open and Steve and Sammy stumbled in arm in arm. Their laughter was immediately cut short as a bowl of Cornflakes hit the wall behind them, followed by a spoon that clunked off Steve's forehead, a carton of milk that sprayed them both in white froth as it spun through the air, and a sugar bowl that not only smashed the already receding joviality but signalled to Steve that now would be a good time for a rapid retreat.

Sammy's *official* other half gave chase, pursuing Steve along the fifth floor corridor and past a startled queue of aged German holidaymakers at reception who had just disembarked from their coach to enjoy some tropical peace and quiet. The fact that the Argentinean was dressed in nothing but Power Rangers boxer shorts did little to dampen his enthusiasm for a fight. In fact the lack of clothes seemed to increase his sense of urgency as by the time Steve had crossed the car park and was rushing down the steps towards the Smugglers, Argentina was only a whisker behind the UK.

Cheered on by the timeshare reps drinking vodka and coffee at Bar Arancha, the duo completed several more loops – down one set of steps, along the railings, then back up the other set of steps – before the Argentinean gave up. He leaned on the railings, body heaving up and down as he tried to suck in air.

'You're fucking dead, you lousy Englishman!' he shouted down at Steve, who, now a good half lap ahead, took the opportunity to grab a breather himself. 'I'll have your balls for breakfast!'

He didn't achieve his culinary ambitions, mainly because Steve disappeared back down to Anthony's for more than a week, biding his time until word got back to him that any life-changing surgery in the nether regions had been postponed due to his pursuer having left for Argentina again.

Despite Sammy having tried to convince her long-distance partner that nothing had happened, she found herself at the wrong end of a Latin backhander. When he left, she packed up her belongings (along with most of his) and moved in with Steve at my mum and stepfather's apartment for a few days.

JOE CAWLEY

CHAPTER FOUR

Steve's band had secured a regular gig at an out-of-town party venue and they invited me to do a guest spot on the drums, which was nice. Actually it was more than nice, it was spectacularly immense. I was due to stand in for two songs – 'Teenage Kicks' by the Undertones and 'All Right Now' by Free, both of which had always featured in my drumming repertoire, no matter which band I happened to be keeping the beat for.

It was more than a chance to revisit my long-forgotten and oft-missed old friend who went by the name of Irresponsibility. It was also an opportunity to maybe ignite a spark of interest and admiration from Joy, and for that reason alone the day couldn't arrive fast enough.

The club was in Buzanada, a town located 4 miles inland from the main resorts. Like many conurbations loosely linked to the southern resorts, its lack of identifiable character matched the desert-like surroundings. Thoughtlessly designed buildings were haphazardly grouped into random complexes that added man-made eyesores to an already ugly scab of dust and rocks.

The ground floor of a warehouse had been converted into a venue on a budget that would have seen change from a £20 note. Outside, broken pallets were stacked against the wall on one side, while the other was home to either a scrap yard or garage mechanic, it was hard to tell.

If the outside was a touch on the insalubrious side, stepping into the cavernous interior was a shock to all the senses, even for those that didn't shock easily. It was like Dante's Inferno, but with everybody wearing shorts and T-shirts rather than horns and tails. Holiday companies such as Buddies and 18–30s charged a set fee for a 'Party in the Hills' excursion that catered for the young, reckless and pliable. After herding everybody together in one of the downtown bars, they would urge the crowd to consume cheap shots and pints of stomach-peeling cocktails, round them up into buses and then let them loose in this house of fun. At the venue they'd be driven into a frenzy by over-excited DJs, indulge in a riotous assembly and ultimately throw up either in the club, on the bus home or, more often than not, over each other.

The sickly stench of beer-sodden clothing and pools of vomit did little to dilute the amorous vibe of the teenage hedonists. Free jugs of sangria and beer were delivered non-stop to long benches where at least one couple would be involved in sexual congress atop the MDF while other pairings exchanged drunken slaps over some petty alcohol-inspired disagreement – both scenes were encouraged with equal and hearty enthusiasm.

Horns blared, spotlights glared and tribal chants emanated from every corner. I expected it to kick off any second and decided the only way to quell the nerves was to join in the spirit as quickly as damn possible.

While the band were setting up backstage, Joy and I fought our way to the toilets, though where the toilets stopped and the main room started had become a little blurred, with as many youngsters in a state of undress on the public side as there were behind the privacy of the blue and pink cubicle doors.

We picked our way back out between the bodies and grabbed a plastic jug of flat, warm beer before elbowing our way into a bench seat close to the front of the stage. Before long the lights dimmed and a voice boomed over the PA system.

'Ladies and gentlemen… are you having a good time?' A communal wave of cheering surfed round the room then broke into a colossal riot of whistling and whooping. 'I didn't hear you. I said… are you having a good time?' continued the DJ, presumably deaf. The deluge of noise was overwhelming, echoing off all four flaking plaster walls. 'Would you please welcome on stage… all the way from England… Kicked!'

Spotlights of a dozen different hues hit the stage, illuminating Steve and the band in stripes of colour as they burst into Bryan Adams' 'Summer of 69', changing the lyrics into 'summer of 94' – to great effect, it has to be said.

By the third song, 'Love Shack', the whole venue was jumping, including Joy, who had climbed onto a table already straining under the weight of a dozen others. Steve looked over and smiled. I gave a thumbs-up and he blew a kiss, which I thought a bit odd then realised it was meant for Joy, who was flailing her arms above her head.

Not one for public displays of emotion, I left Joy to dance alone; I was happy to see her letting herself go and secretly gloated that Steve had singled us out for attention amid the thousands of nubile half-dressed girls who had staggered their way to the front of the stage to ogle and presumably volunteer their services should the occasion present itself.

My nerves grew as the band played the final chorus of 'Born to be Wild', the cue for me to get ready to go on stage. As the cheering died down, I readied myself. But instead of the call, Steve burst straight into the next song, and then the next, and the next, until I knew it was nearly time for them to stop. I tried to catch his attention in what I hoped wasn't a desperate gesture, but he had his eyes closed, strumming the low-strung bass and nodding his head to the beat.

'I think he's forgotten about me getting up,' I shouted up to Joy, tugging on the hem of her red mini-dress.

'Eh?' she shouted back, still gyrating to a rocked-up version of 'Do Ya Think I'm Sexy'.

I mimed drumming, pointed to myself and then to the stage. Joy gave a little wave to Steve then gestured down at me and did the same drumming mime. Steve nodded and winked back.

As the song finished, he swiped a black shirt sleeve across his face to clear the sweat and grabbed the microphone.

'We've got to finish soon, but before we do, I want to invite a good friend of mine to play the drums. Give a cheer for Joe…'

The crowd looked round and cheered as I walked to the stage as nonchalantly as my surging adrenaline would allow. Steve high-fived me. I grabbed the sticks from the drummer and sat down behind the kit. He gave me a nod. I clicked the sticks together in a four-count and the band exploded into the Undertones' 'Teenage Kicks'.

Halfway through the song I relaxed, remembering to enjoy the moment. The crowd at the front of the stage – mostly girls – were bouncing up and down in unison, still transfixed by Steve. He turned round and beamed, rocking his head up and down. As in every gig, I spotted a handful of faces fixed on my playing – wannabe drummers, dreaming of being up there on stage, like many boys do at some point in their lives. Their attention spurred on my own drumming as I hit the skins with just a little more force.

I was in ecstasy, locked in one of those magical plateaus of complete harmony that every band member experiences on stage every once in a while. Having seen Joy enjoying the night so much, I felt compelled to share my own moment with her. Through the smoky haze I could see she was still dancing on the table, which was now packed with even more drunken bodies throwing their limbs around in a similar fashion.

I smiled in her direction but, like the vast majority, she was watching Steve climb on top of the speaker stack at the side of the stage. He nodded to bring the song to an end, leapt into the air and landed just as I smashed two cymbals in a final beat. Frenzied cheering erupted, even Joy was punching the air and whooping.

Steve thanked me through the microphone as I regained my place below Joy, who still hadn't noticed my return. Thoroughly buzzed-up from drumming, I needed a drink and shouted up to Joy to see if she wanted a refill, but she was completely immersed in the live music.

The band played their last song while I got

drunker and drunker. As Steve left the stage, he blew kisses to the girls at the front who were still screaming for more, then pointed at Joy and me and blew another.

When the night eventually finished, both Joy and I had glazed eyes. Admittedly mine were glazed from having ingested far more alcohol than would be deemed healthy by anyone with even a smidgeon of sense. Joy however had only had a couple of beers, yet her big brown eyes sparkled wide, mesmerised.

It was one of many befuddled thoughts that vied for attention as we headed for the exit, but not the most pressing one. That honour belonged to the desperate realisation that I was about to be very sick. And before I had time to engage my limbs into doing the sensible thing – in other words, shuffling to somewhere more discreet – I threw up all down my front, across most of Joy's back, and a little bit in the hair of a girl who had chosen to sit down at the precise spot where I had decided to hurl. A 'little bit' was 'a lot more' than she was expecting, which she conveyed in an explosion of vitriol the like of which is usually reserved for the kind of people who steal children or beat old ladies about the head with heavy objects.

Needless to say I was in no fit state to argue my case. I held my hands up and nodded in agreement at the new titles I was being bestowed with. Joy grabbed my hand, told the girl to go fuck herself, and hurried me away to a waiting taxi. I was touched. I think. Then promptly fell asleep on her shoulder on the ride home.

I'd like to say it was an innate sense that Joy

wasn't by my side that woke me up in the middle of the night. But it wasn't. It was blinding pain. My brain hammered the inside of my skull with each pulse of blood. Joy's absence only came to my attention as I got up to track down a bottle of life-saving Paracetamols. I knew we had some in the mirrored cabinet above the bathroom sink. Problem was, no matter how hard I tried to make progress towards the door, the 45-degree slope of the floor made any attempts at walking in a straight line futile. After a couple of tries my forehead bounced off the wardrobe and I ricocheted back onto the bed.

'Sorry,' I muttered, feeling around to see if I'd caused injury to Joy. But I hadn't, because she wasn't there. Which was a little sobering. But not much. And as I pondered where she might actually be in this crazy spinning world, I was fully aware that I hadn't a hope in hell of actually making it out of the bedroom. Gaining strange comfort from this thought, I fell right back into a deep, drunken, slobbering slumber.

JOE CAWLEY

CHAPTER FIVE

Obviously hangovers are par for the course for those foolish enough to invest their entire time and wealth in bar life. At least that's what I was telling myself as I forced down a dry Weetabix in a bid to stop the retching and pangs of guilt that are part and parcel of morning afters.

They weren't the only feelings I had that particular morning though. It was 8.45am, fifteen minutes before we needed to start prepping and shopping for a busy August day, and Joy was still nowhere to be seen.

I headed down to the bar, hoping nobody would shout down a cheery greeting from one of the El Beril balconies and force me to lift my head. If I kept it perfectly still, the throbbing was containable.

The bar was unlocked when I got there and Joy was already busy in the kitchen. A pan of potatoes was frothing in sea salt while wafts of chicken leaked from the oven and mixed with the chemical perfume of bug spray – pre-emptive strikes to keep the little buggers away from the food.

'Morning. Salad still needs doing,' she said brightly, pointing an oven glove at the fridge.

First things first, I reached for the first-aid box. 'Erm… where were you last night?' I said.

'You were in a right state. I didn't fancy you being sick on me again, so I slept on Steve's sofa.'

'Oh,' I replied, not altogether pleased with the notion but currently lacking the resilience to continue the conversation. 'Right, I'm off to do the shop. Catch you later.'

As I turned off the motorway for Los Cristianos the traffic ground to a halt. Two cars had touched bumpers at the roundabout entrance and both drivers were arguing the toss over whose fault it was. I looked around at my fellow drivers. Like me, most were groggy-eyed and reckless-haired, their ability to appreciate the delights of the Canarian morning still several cups of coffee away. Others however displayed an alertness and smartness that suggested they were most definitely morning people.

People are different, of that there's no doubt, and one of the best places to observe those differences is an early morning traffic jam, before pretences and fantasy have had time to temper their appearance.

One of the most common character types seen at this time is 'the Stressed'. The car in front is a Toyota. In it, a man in a suit is already doing business before he's even reached the office. A mobile phone is tucked under a tilted head, a long antenna protrudes from behind his neck while arms gesticulate to a distant colleague. If there's one thing worse than floaty bits in your morning coffee, it's someone else hitting you with a morning stress call. At this time of the day a brain should have nothing more to concern itself with than the business of breathing in and breathing out and making sure that you don't pour orange juice on your cornflakes.

The phone user winds his window up as the melee from the car alongside – a rusty white Peugeot – threatens to drown out his conversation. Within the Peugeot slumps a representative of 'the

Beleaguered'. An unshaven father stares forlornly ahead as four young children hold a tag-wrestling competition on the rear seat, causing the car to rock and sway. Despite the din, his head starts to loll forward, but he jolts awake as the traffic moves on and he slowly rolls out of view to allow the next genus to draw level – 'the Raver'.

There are only two things worse than floaty bits in your coffee this early in the day and those are an early morning stress call and explosive techno music booming out at number eleven on the volume dial. This black nightclub on wheels is also rocking and swaying, but through the smoked-glass windows I can just make out the figure of a boy raving at 164 beats per minute. He looks no older than fourteen. The car has been converted into as much of a disco as is possible without having to charge an entrance fee and employ bouncers to stand outside. The young driver notices I'm staring and lowers his sunglasses momentarily before continuing to drum frantically on the steering wheel. I feel exhausted just watching.

In front, a young woman displaying all the characteristics of 'the Late' is using the time to finish off her hair, encouraging it to sit down in the places where it was standing up and stand up in the places where it was sitting down. After a compromise she carefully starts to apply some lippy and in my grouchy state I'm tempted to nudge her car as the car in front of her pulls away, but I don't. After she's painted her mouth, she moves on to eyelashes, still ignoring the beeping from impatient drivers behind me.

You can never tell if someone is looking straight

at you through the rear-view mirror but you can if they have their head out of the window and are beaming broadly in your direction, as is 'the Flirter', the passenger in the white builder's van that has pulled alongside the woman making up her face. There are no subtle tactics here, just a toot-toot and a sound that you would more usually employ to befriend a hesitant kitten. Obviously used to the attention, the woman throws a disdainful glance at the builder and his mate and continues with her mascara while the van moves slowly on and repeats the performance with the next female driver, and the next.

And me? More often than not I'm the one with a shirt buttoned unevenly, looking like 'the Ragged', pretending to be 'the Alert' and trying my best to be 'the Ignored'. The morning type I really want to be though is 'the In Bed'. If there are three things worse than floaty bits in your coffee, they're early morning stress calls, deafening dance music and being scrutinised at daft o'clock when you've got a raging hangover. Roll on the afternoon siesta.

~

Pushing the flatbed cart up and down the narrow aisles of the cash and carry, I nodded at all the usual faces – baggy-eyed bar and restaurant owners, restocking after another late night pandering to the carefree and leisured.

It's often said that it's every man's dream to own his own bar and play the jovial landlord always ready with a clever quip and hearty banter for his flock of regulars. Tenerife seems to be the Fantasy

Island of the hospitality trade, with thousands arriving each year to try their hand as bar proprietor. A few stay, but many, like us, being totally unprepared for a life behind bars, find that either the heat, the commitment, the administrative battles, or being bitten by their own dog – the booze – cuts short their aspirations and leads to heartache, either financial or emotional; often both. The landlord flirts with his young barmaid, the wife runs off with the Dorada delivery man and the *hacienda* (tax office) sends an invitation to pay off the telephone-number-sized debts that were conveniently ignored by the previous seven bar owners.

The chirpy landlord will joke about these trivialities whilst propping up the bar late at night, becoming his own worst customer. But inside, the excessive volume of alcohol churns up an explosive mixture of anger and frustration ready to be unleashed on the next unsuspecting checkout girl at the cash and carry who overcharges him yet again for a 10-pound can of Heinz beans. If you can handle this kind of strife and still smile at your customers, then maybe a life in one of this sub-tropical nirvana's watering holes will provide all that you desire and deserve; in which case, good luck to you. If, however, that activation of the facial muscles that push the corners of your mouth northwards is as rare as a toilet seat in the Veronicas nightlife strip, then perhaps the dream should remain just that.

One Spanish veteran of the cash-and-carry run always had the look of a man on the edge. Obviously not a great believer in mirrors, he sported clumps of thick black hair that leapt in all directions as if trying to flee. On this particular morning, just the three bottom buttons of his pale denim shirt had been employed, albeit in mismatching holes. His eyes were blood-red and wide, perhaps forced open by copious amounts of caffeine or pieces of invisible tape. An unlit cigarette dangled from his bottom lip, pointing first up then down as he mumbled to himself, clattering into shelves and other trolleys and blindly snatching at various tins and boxes, on autopilot, then tossing them on his cart with a good deal of disdain.

I wondered if this is what I'd become if I stayed in the bar trade, totally disinterested in my appearance, a complete slave to the bar and repeating the same routines on autopilot day in, day out. I shuddered at the thought. Then shuddered again at an even more alarming thought. I'd forgotten to grab the money from the safe. Idiot!

I scanned the half-full trolley, calculating how much it would cost. I *did* have some personal money with me, but probably not enough. I thought about putting back the cellophane-wrapped flowers I'd selected as an apology to Joy but decided to see if I could get away with another money-saving tactic – rearranging some of the more expensive items so the checkout girl couldn't see them. Thankfully she expended her usual amount of effort on scanning my cart, and with no more than a quick glance, staying glued to her chair, she presented me with a bill for less than half what it should have been.

Mario, our predecessor at the Smugglers, had initiated us into this practice on our first trip to the cash and carry, three years ago. He showed us how to stack the shopping cart so that certain items weren't visible unless the checkout girl actually descended from her mighty three-legged throne and picked things up, which was highly unusual. At first we were shocked at such underhand and dishonest tactics, but as he had quite rightly pointed out, 'The amount of times they flickin' overcharge you, you have to get it back somehows.'

~

The sun had broken free of the anvil-shaped Roque del Conde mountain, bathing Los Cristianos and the coastline in a golden light. Alongside the motorway, palm trees cast long shadows across the bleach-white new-build villas on the left. Beyond them the sunlight caught the Atlantic waves, sparks bouncing off the blue crests like machine-gun fire.

I wound both front windows down, allowing a warm stream of air to flow through my hair. Finally my hangover was lifting. To my right, the mountains of the south rose sharply, their slopes patched green with banana plantations and vine terraces and peppered with white smallholdings and pale grey clusters of half-finished apartment blocks. High up, the razor-sharp summits slashed the cloudless sky with a serrated ridge that stretched from north to south as far as the eye could see.

It was as perfect a summer's day as you could get in Tenerife. Heading down the coast road to El Beril, towards the sparkling ocean, I smiled to myself and stretched a hand out into the rushing breeze.

By the time I arrived back I was in fine spirits. There wasn't enough time to return to the cash and carry before opening up, but scanning the items in the back of the car I figured we'd be okay for most things during the day. I laid the flowers on the box of oranges and carried them down the steps to the Smugglers. The doors were still closed and the patio chairs had not yet been put out, which was unusual as it was one of the first things that Joy did in the morning, a ploy to let newcomers know that we'd be opening soon.

Balancing on one leg, I flicked open the door with my other foot and went inside. As I walked towards the kitchen, I noticed that the bar was still not laid out with bar towels and the condiment sets on the tables still hadn't been filled; the bottles of oil and vinegar were still smeared and half empty. Strange, I thought as I walked into the kitchen. Maybe Joy had had to nip back to the apartment for something, but it was a bit odd that she'd left the door open and unlocked. Either way, it wouldn't diminish the effect of me presenting her with my bouquet of apology.

And then my world collapsed.

CHAPTER SIX

Joy stood with her back to me; the curved rainbow of colours on her striped hot pants caught my eye first. I opened my mouth to ask about the prepping but before the words came out my brain registered something very wrong with the scene. A hand rested on Joy's backside. Her arms were wrapped round somebody sitting on the freezer, her head on his chest. That somebody was Steve.

My muscles tensed, heart pounded. Nausea rose as my insides started to burn. The box of oranges dropped to the floor as Steve caught sight of me. He pushed Joy aside. She spun round. Her eyes shot wide.

'Alright, mate,' smiled Steve. He pretended as if nothing had happened.

'Oh God!' rasped Joy. 'Oh God.'

I turned around and walked out. I was lost for words. My mind raced out of control, whirling to try and make sense of what I had just seen. I stormed behind the bar to wash the few glasses that were still in the sink, subconsciously seeking comfort in a familiar task. The heat rose in my cheeks. My eyes stung, temples pulsing as if about to explode.

I longed for normality. In the bar the *real* world hadn't changed. Beads of condensation clung to the stainless steel beer tap; the mahogany-brown bar top still bore the same marks and scratches it had had the day we walked in; table seven still had the crack in the glass where I had spread-eagled Joy during a playful bout of romance in the early days.

Steve was first out of the kitchen. He sat and faced me across the bar. 'You okay?'

Silence.

'Don't worry, mate, it's not what it looked like. Joy was just a bit…'

I lifted my gaze from the sink. 'I think you'd better leave.'

Steve paused, opened his mouth, then closed it again and left in silence. I looked across to the kitchen. Joy still hadn't come out. I didn't want to ever go back in that kitchen, scene of the crime, but I knew I had to. I strode towards the doorway shaking uncontrollably, shock jolting my body and mind with surges of adrenaline ready for the confrontation.

Oranges dotted the terracotta tiles. A blue ring of flame still danced merrily under a pan of potatoes that expelled a column of steam into the dull grey extractor hood.

Joy was still leaning on the freezer, facing out now. She watched me come in, eyes agog. Both hands cupped her mouth as if trying to forestall a scream. The small diamond eternity ring I had presented to her on her first birthday in Tenerife sparkled on her slender fingers. It was my symbol of commitment to show that I fully intended to spend the rest of my days with her even though we'd both said we didn't see the point in getting married. 'Why fix it if it's not broke' we'd both agreed.

I stared, breathing heavily. I hadn't a clue what to do. So many thoughts, so many questions, so many unfamiliar emotions.

'What…? How…?' I struggled to get the words

out, my lips started to tremble.

Joy's shoulders juddered up and down. 'I'm sorry. I'm *so* sorry,' she blubbered. Her damp eyes searched mine for signs of what would come next.

A tear trickled down my cheek. 'How long has it been going on?' I croaked.

'It just happened.'

'How long?'

'I didn't mean to hurt you, Joe.'

'How long?' A little louder this time.

'A few weeks,' she said, shifting her gaze to the floor.

A few weeks! The burning intensified again, words erupting in a fury. 'Have you slept with him?'

Joy's eyes flicked up at mine, filling with tears again. She nodded.

'How many times?' The questions were flowing out of control now. What difference did it make if she'd slept with him once, a hundred times? The trust, the intimacy, the respect, the relationship... it was broken now.

'How could you? How could you do that to me?'

'I'm sorry.'

'With *him*, my best friend.'

'It just happened.'

'It didn't *just* happen. You two made it fucking happen. These things don't *just* happen.'

'I didn't mean to hurt you, I promise.'

'Hurt me? Hurt me? That's not even close.' I'd come right into the kitchen now and picked the chopping knife off the square table in the middle of the room, jabbing the point towards her. 'You've wrecked me – us. You've wrecked this, you've wrecked everything.'

51

Joy reeled back. Her eyes widened further as she peered down at the steel blade flashing inches from her stomach.

I put the blade down. 'Get out. Just fuck off. GET OUT!'

Joy left quickly. I stared at the spot where she'd been standing. What *was* I going to do? I couldn't think and slipped back into autopilot. I picked up the knife again and continued to prepare the salad for the day's meals, rhythmically chopping at a cucumber. What the hell *was* I going to do?

After finishing in the kitchen, I moved to the bar chores. Joy was still there, having quietly carried on getting the place ready. The bar *must* come first, of course! As the wall clock ticked 10.30, with scary professionalism she took a deep breath, dried her eyes one more time and greeted our first guests. I disappeared back into the kitchen, completely unable to deal with talking to anyone.

Her ability to mask her emotions and carry on as normal while in the public eye both worried and amazed me. If she was that adept at deception, how well had I ever really known her? How long had she really been seeing Steve behind my back, the two of them keeping their dirty little secret from me?

The first order came in. Joy wrote on the order sheet stuck to the fridge: '2 full breakfasts, 1 no tomato extra beans'. I was thankful for something to take my mind off the suffocating mix of heartbreak, anger and disbelief.

More orders flooded in, silently conveyed in blue wipe-able ink. In a moment of respite, I watched Joy laughing with a family of four as she collected their plates. Unbelievable! She brought the plates into the kitchen, placing them on the counter and taking care not to catch my eye. She'd switched me off, my grief invisible to her. I was now nothing more than an inconvenience in her sordid affair.

My anger switched to Steve. How was I going to deal with that bastard? I'd never been the violent type and even now I couldn't see any benefit in smashing in his face. We'd been through a lot together. Many times I'd been there for him when he'd been on the receiving end of verbal lashings from previous girlfriends.

Four years earlier he'd been the one who'd provided just the right amount of comfort on the night I found out my dad had taken his own life, thousands of miles away in America. Visibly upset himself, he gave me a physical shoulder to cry on and made sure I didn't spend too much time on my own mourning, always making himself available. Now it all meant nothing.

Perhaps that had been an act of deceit too. Perhaps he and Joy had shared secret moments back then too. God knows, there were plenty of occasions when I'd left them alone in the house together. I knew Joy found him physically attractive, she'd told me he was good-looking, always with the tag-on 'but not as much as you'. Right, sure. That meant nothing either. I'd been deceived good and proper. Stupidity joined the stew of emotions that churned inside.

My mind replayed scenes from the previous few weeks to see if there was anything I should have spotted, anything I could have done to stop this happening. Of course, it all seemed so obvious now: insinuations, looks, and Joy's desire to include

Steve in everything we did. The gig. Joy fixated on his singing. Not being there when I woke up. Sleeping on Steve's settee… Oh you fucking idiot, Joe!

As I was mulling over how stupid I'd been, I spotted Steve returning to the bar, just as Joy brought more plates for me to wash.

'Tell Steve I want to speak to him,' I said.

After a couple of minutes he sauntered in, still bearing a smile of denial.

'What's up, mate?'

'You're barred. Don't ever step foot in this bar again. Oh, and get the fuck out of my mum's apartment.'

It was the only control I had over him, and I seriously doubted that he cared. I looked into his icy blue eyes. There were no signs of apology, just a wry smile. Now it was out in the open he had no need to hide the fact that he saw me as the enemy. But that conceited sneer was to let me know he'd won. He'd come into my life invited, bulldozed the cosy path I'd been treading and snatched my girlfriend.

The rest of the shift passed in a blur, without a word being spoken between Joy and me. David arrived with Sammy at two o'clock to take over.

'You okay, bruv?'

I slammed down the cutlery I'd been washing and tore off my apron.

'No, not really. I just found out Joy's been having an affair with Steve.'

'Shit! You're joking!'

David lit a cigarette as he always did in stressful situations. At that moment Joy dumped another pile of dirty plates on the kitchen top.

'*You* bitch,' he hissed, with more venom than I'd ever seen him use, even with me.

I was taken with his protectiveness, but still felt a pang of pity to see Joy the subject of such hate. I doubted Joy had ever been hated by anybody in her whole life until then. It must have been a new experience for her and I wondered if the animosity had stirred any feelings of regret. She took a deep breath, then turned and left.

'What are you going to do?' asked David.

I shrugged, staring at the tiles. 'Better go and talk to her, I suppose.'

CHAPTER SEVEN

Joy's tears had stopped by the time I'd walked back to the apartment. She stood behind the ironing board trying to make a dent in the pile of T-shirts and shorts stacked on the arm of our sofa-bed in the living room. The sound of children playing on the beach carried through the open patio doors and the long cotton curtains stirred in the brisk sea breeze. The curtain top began to billow like a sail as the bottom half, restrained by a rope tie-back, scuffed at the floor like a petulant child.

'Need anything doing for tonight?' asked Joy without looking up.

'How could you do that to me?'

Joy placed the iron upright on the edge of the tattered yellow cover and tucked a stray strand of fringe behind her ear. Her eyes bored into me, black and intense.

'You think it's all about you, don't you? You think the whole world revolves around you. Well, what about me? What about my life?'

She jabbed a finger at me as the words grew louder. I stepped in and closed the door, aware that the ensuing argument would snake along all the pathways of the complex, finding open windows and doors through which to spread its poison.

'I have *no* life. My life is for everybody else. I'm at everybody's beck and call in the bar, I'm at *your* beck and call in here. You and David treat me like I'm just staff, I have no real friends, no social life, nothing. How do you think that makes me feel, Joe?'

57

'I…'

'I have *nothing* of my own – apart from this… with Steve. It's mine, it's my choice, under my control…' Joy was sobbing again now, big fat tears of despair. It seemed she truly felt she was the victim in all this.

'So you're carrying on? It's not over? You're saying that this is it for me and you? Just like that?' I said, flabbergasted.

This was not the confrontation that I had expected. I thought there'd be regret, sympathy and talk of 'how it would never happen again'. Battered and bemused, I opened the door and walked out, shaking my head.

~

Although we still hadn't been able to make much use of the beach, the new paved promenade that ran in front of El Beril provided the perfect place to ponder life, staring across the waves at the island of La Gomera, and it was here that I sat on a stone step and gazed out to sea.

It was the same place that Joy and I had regularly sat at night during our first year abroad while we were floating in our good fortune at having found such a perfect place to live. I could still smell the aroma of fried food, cigarette smoke and stale beer that was embedded in our clothes and hair, blended with the fading scent of Joy's perfume. Our foreheads greasy with sweat, eyes blackened with exhaustion and lips dry from the long hours in energy-sapping heat – these were the trophies of our hard work, determination and cooperation, proof of another hard night's work, successfully completed together.

We might have had a horrific night in the bar – slapping Friedhelm, our loyal, baggy-jowled German patron, on the back to stop him choking on a pork chop; peeling Buster the cat off the face of a dog that had had the misfortune to stray into the bar; or, for Joy, avoiding the lecherous advances of the growing number of Spanish builders who were using Smugglers as their second home.

However bad things might have been at the time, sitting on this step, holding hands and looking out across the moonlit ocean, all of our troubles would melt away as we glugged on cold bottles of beer at three in the morning. We would savour the night's silence and watch the halo of pale yellow hover over neon-lit Las Américas in the distance while specks of light from a dozen fishing boats winked from the black expanse of ocean ahead. The two sides of Tenerife: one frenetic and messy, the other uncomplicated and calm. Just like working in the Smugglers and spending time on this step.

There were plenty of worse places to make a living, we'd agree back then, and Joy would snuggle in closer until the buzz from work finally gave way to the need for sleep.

I picked up a smooth flat pebble and spun it into the water, watching the ripples expand then fade away. At first I'd figured something similar would happen with Joy. A big splash as her affair was outed, followed by ripples of pain that would gradually peter out as life got back to normal. But it seemed I'd got that wrong. Joy had no intention of stopping. This wasn't just a case of two-timing, it was also her dumping me for my best friend. The end of a lifelong relationship.

I couldn't envisage life without her. We'd done so much, been together since our earliest days at nursery school when she'd pushed me off the slide. We had been a close team at junior school, watching each other's backs, had opined on respective teenage romances like brother and sister and, almost inevitably, had become an item when our adolescent hormones collided. Maybe we'd come full circle, maybe the ride was always going to come to an end. Even so, I couldn't in a million years have imagined that it would finish like this.

Joy hadn't just ripped the relationship apart, she'd ripped me apart. She was part of me; she had the outgoing carefree personality I longed to have; she was the friendly, full of love person I wanted to be. She had become my personality, just as the bar had become hers. Without her I felt bare and exposed, stripped of importance and drained of colour.

I felt I should have the upper hand, standing as I was on higher moral ground, but in truth it was Joy who held all the cards. Despite my anger, I knew I still wanted her back. But she didn't want me.

~

For the next few days we played musical chairs with apartments. Joy had been entrusted with the keys to several properties whose owners who would call on her every now and then to check that their holiday home hadn't been flooded or broken into. Despite the opportunity to participate in one of the island's common 'management' scams – letting out properties without the owner's knowledge and pocketing the money oneself – Joy had always been honest to a fault. In fact she provided this service free of charge, leaving herself at the beck and call of over-anxious second-home-owners at any time of the day or night.

Joy had been extra vigilant about not letting any keys out of her sight since our dealings with the Czechoslovakian squatters in our first few months. Back then, acting in good faith to help out a distressed stranger, we had found ourselves embroiled in a full-blown scam that eventually involved court orders, hitmen and half of El Beril working in unison to reclaim a friend's hijacked apartment that Joy had innocently rented out for a few days.

She wasn't so circumspect now, though, when it came to Steve's accommodation needs. And so it was that he moved out of my mum's apartment into one of the front-line bungalows overlooking the ocean while I packed an overnight bag and moved into my mum's. Unfortunately, without telling me, Joy had also packed a bag and moved into another apartment in the Altamira, leaving Buster the cat the single and rather lonely tenant of Number 85. The next day I moved back in.

David suggested I take a few days off so I finally managed to spend time on the beach, practising a little lilo philosophy. Floating a hundred yards from shore on a fluorescent pink blow-up, I tried to make sense of all that had happened, and more importantly, what should happen next.

Around me, families threw balls, splashed in the

surf and strolled along the water's edge. Dashes and stripes from parasols and beach towels streaked the golden canvas like the random brushstrokes of an infant artist. Young couples played bat and ball, tossed Frisbees and embraced in a tangle of arms and legs.

It was as perfect a scene of holiday happiness as could be found anywhere, but little did these holidaymakers realise that in their vacation paradise real lives were played out just like at home. Unlike the postcards, buckets and spades and sunbeds on the beach, workers weren't just props in the theatre of the holiday resort. Little did they know, nor rightly care, that painted smiles glossed over the cracks, that behind the scenes the receptionists, cleaners and bar staff had their own personal traumas, traumas that to holidaymakers were inconsequential compared with their duty to provide softer mattresses, brighter bathroom bulbs and pints of beer that were filled right to the top.

Lying on my stomach, resting my chin on the back of my hands, I savoured the scene as the gentle roll of the water slopped quietly against the edge of the lilo. I felt like running away. Behind lay Las Américas; on the other side of the island was Africa. The world really could be my oyster – if I wasn't so trapped. Trapped in a debt of £165,000. Trapped in a job that I didn't care for and that didn't satisfy me. Trapped in a situation where the pleasure of spending twenty-four hours a day with the one I loved had now become a living nightmare.

Jack, my stepfather, who had lent us some of the money and helped to arrange a mortgage for the rest, had insisted that it was written into the contract that if anybody decided to walk away from the bar they would forfeit the right to a share of its worth or profits. That was the only hold I had over Joy, but now the money was inconsequential. The pressing matter was what the heck I was going to do about Joy and Steve. Should I stand by and let it run its course? Should I bugger off and leave them to it? Should I fight and try to win her back? At that very moment, with the sun warming my back, the waves rocking me like a baby, I would have been quite happy for the ocean to carry me away to its silent realm. But, instead, I paddled back to shore to get ready for my first shift with Joy.

JOE CAWLEY

CHAPTER EIGHT

'You okay to work?' asked David as we swapped places in the kitchen.

'Yeah… Better just get it over with,' I said. He gave me a brotherly hug, a gesture made more meaningful by its rarity.

It was going to be strange working so close to Joy, knowing that we had turned from lifelong lovers to enemies in such a dizzyingly short space of time. *How* difficult was something that I had underestimated on a grand scale. For her I was an inconvenience at best. Where once there had been compassion and love, there was now simply bland indifference to my feelings.

The physical, spiritual and psychological effects of new love, or lust, as I considered it – though actually I would have preferred not to think about it at all – were powerful, almost hallucinatory. The things that Joy had previously held close to her heart had been cast out, along with logic. I mean how logical was it that for nigh on twenty-two years I had been one of the most important people in her life, only to become suddenly irrelevant, even though I hadn't changed or done anything?

Every time I caught sight of her talking, laughing, carrying on as normal, the knives of rejection, incomprehension, jealousy, anger, betrayal and longing twisted their sordid blades ever deeper.

Even three days on after having found them together in the kitchen, my emotions danced from one negative state to another without warning. It was draining. It was madness, similar to the madness that must have possessed Joy to throw away everything we had built up over the years for that lowlife scumbag who had been lying and pretending ever since he arrived. I hated him. I hated her. At least in that moment. By the time I'd cleared the empty plates off table five I loved her again. After I'd added them to the growing pile of soiled crockery next to the sink hate had returned and I wanted her to see my pain.

We had a break in kitchen orders so I untied my white apron and sat dejectedly at the bar.

'What are you looking so miserable about?' said a customer as he waited at the till to pay. 'Got a face like a slapped arse. Can't be that bad – at least it's sunny!'

Even though the holidaymakers were unaware of our relationship turmoil, several of the residents had found out. Some, like Frank, were direct in their advice. 'Been dumped for that flash twat then, have you? Why don't you just get hold of a good piece of four-be-two and beat the living crap out of him?'

Most were a little more subtle in their digging for dirt, such as Supermarket Patricia. 'Is he a good friend of yours, that Steve, only... now, don't get me wrong, I could be completely mistaken... it's just that he seems to be getting a little... how can I put it... *close* to Joy?'

Although admittedly my judgement was clouded at that time, it appeared that the residents who knew about our situation could be divided into two camps. There were those who were genuinely sad to see us split up – namely my brother David; Barry, the former flight attendant turned policeman turned

Smugglers quiz master and occasional bar help; and a very small handful of others – and those who revelled in this juicy new bit of El Beril gossip.

Boredom amongst the Brit residents of El Beril – though I'm sure the same applies in all expat communities – was a common problem. Not necessarily for those who were experiencing the boredom, but rather for those around them, who would often became implicated in fabricated scandal and dramas, just for something to occupy the time between mid-morning gin and tonics and afternoon siestas. In the bar, I felt that not only was I perceived as a loser in this whole scenario, but also that others were taking delight in the misery it was causing, an eagerly observed soap-opera episode in their otherwise mundane lives.

Behind the bar that day, Joy was yet again trying to ignore the drunken murmurings of two Spanish workmen who had decided to spend their afternoon break comforted by the cool sensation of Dorada beer rather than the soothing touch of a cotton pillow. They were part of a team of a dozen or so who had been imported from northern Spain to work on the construction of a new hotel next to the Altamira. When they first arrived they were the height of politeness, keen to ingratiate themselves with those at the centre of the local community – in other words, the bar owners. Over time, however, boredom and frustration at being away from their families for such a long stretch seemed to have turned them into a bunch of naughty schoolchildren; they began bickering amongst themselves and generally causing havoc whenever they appeared en masse.

While we appreciated their regular custom, both for alcohol and for regular feeding, we'd already had to ban a handful of them for various misdemeanours – groping Sammy, urinating in the potted plants and on one terrifying occasion pointing a gun at Buster. The latter could be deemed an act of self-defence as admittedly Buster had started the altercation.

Our ginger guard cat had taken an instant dislike to Roberto, a rotund, forty-something man with permanently glazed eyes. Perhaps there was previous history that we hadn't witnessed, but whenever Buster saw Roberto coming down the stairs he would arch his back and howl before the man had even set foot through the door. When he entered the bar, our cat would rake at his ankles with his sturdy claws.

To be fair to Roberto, living in a workman's hut with very few comforts and working on a building site in 40-plus heat had seemingly toughened him against most of what life in El Beril could throw at him, including psychotic cats. At first Buster's antagonism was viewed as a joke by Roberto's workmates, but things became more serious when Buster upped the ante by lying in wait on top of the gas cupboard one afternoon.

I watched Roberto tentatively walk down the steps, his glassy eyes scanning for any impending feline offensive. Noticeably relieved, he put one foot in the doorway – only to be struck in the side of the head by a furry banshee that embedded itself in the poor man's hair like a barbed turban. Roberto and his friends managed to get Buster off, but not before considerable surface damage had been inflicted.

The next time we saw Roberto he had understandably come better prepared, outfitted in steel-toe-capped boots, builder's gloves and a long-sleeved sweatshirt. Intent on employing a pre-emptive strike, he spied Buster asleep between a pair of frail pensioners who, having enjoyed a nice bit of gammon, were confiding in Joy that their greatest wish in life at this current moment was for a nice English cup of tea.

Sitting back with contented smiles, what they were expecting was a familiar hot beverage neatly accompanied by a foil-wrapped biscuit. What was possibly furthest from their mind as they contemplated the welcoming decor of this friendly British bar was an encounter with a facially scarred Spaniard running at them with a gun in his hand.

They froze, but thankfully Buster didn't. He leapt from wall bench to wall bench, hissing as he sprang from the laps of one startled diner after another, before darting into the kitchen.

Frank, the dour truck driver from Oldham, our most loyal patron and regular supplier of disastrous DIY services, jumped off his bar stool to try and wrestle the pistol from Roberto. Even with help from Roberto's Spanish colleague and myself, it was several minutes before he managed to herd the enraged attacker out of the bar.

Roberto never returned, probably more for his own safety than because of anything that we had said. However, his compatriots were quite capable of causing hassle without his help and the two of them sitting at the bar now were clearly annoying

Joy, spilling beer all over the bar top and demanding every ounce of her attention.

For once I didn't jump to Joy's defence, strangely revelling in her frustration at having to fend off their drunken advances. We were no longer speaking. Instead we tried to keep out of each other's way as much as we could in such a confined environment. Joy continued to be her jolly self with the customers, dropping any smiles with a resounding thud as soon as she turned and came into the kitchen. There was a different look about Joy now, a side I hadn't seen in her. It was hard, stone cold, as though I had been her enemy for years. My heart sank further than I thought possible. How on earth were we going to carry on working together? Especially when I knew she was just whiling her time away in the bar, desperate to be rid of me and seek solace in the arms of Steve.

I also got the impression that men were looking at her in a different light now. In my eyes male holidaymakers *and* some of the expats spent longer talking to her on their own, making eye contact, touching her arm. They seemed to regard her as 'available' now, despite the fact that she was actually with Steve. Had it been *that* obvious in the bar before that we were a couple? Was some kind of invisible binding still tangible to those who saw us in the same room together? Or did the fact that Joy had strayed once make her more open to the possibility again? It made me jealous, and it didn't help that Joy clearly deemed it no longer my business to feel or do anything about it, except watch and suffer.

The following few days flew by in a blur,

opposing emotions coming and going as if trapped in an over-oiled rotating door. Then she dropped the next bombshell.

~

We were prepping in the kitchen in our now customary silence, Joy chopping cucumbers, me tenderising chicken fillets.

'Steve's going back to England,' she said suddenly.

'When?' I said. My heart lifted a little.

'Day after tomorrow. Summer season's ended. The gigs are drying up.'

I could feel Joy's eyes boring into me. I looked up. She clutched the knife to her chest.

'I'm going back too.'

The words took a while to make an impact. When they did, it was with a force that I was unprepared for, sucking the breath from my lungs and filling my head with toxic hate.

'We can't carry on like this. It's not fair on you, me *or* Steve,' said Joy, quietly. 'Steve's going back on Tuesday, I'm going back the following Tuesday, to go and live with him.'

'You... you can't,' I spluttered. 'What about the bar? You'll get nothing. What about us? Is there nothing worth saving?'

'We need to get out of here. I owe it to Steve...'

'You owe it to *Steve*? You owe *him*? What about me? Do you not owe *me* a chance?'

But Joy's mind was apparently made up. I had precisely nine days before Joy walked out of my life forever.

CHAPTER NINE

Despite my world having been unceremoniously tipped upside down, the bar continued to demand our full attention, like a spoiled child, doling out a daily succession of new trials and tribulations. The worst of these was the sudden opening of a rival British bar on the other side of the supermarket.

Steve had left for England, providing much relief on the nights I lay awake and alone, staring at the ceiling tortured by thoughts of him and Joy together. But the clock was still painfully ticking away the seconds, minutes, hours and days until Joy would disappear forever. To be honest, any new spanner in the works offered welcome albeit temporary distraction from thinking about Joy's departure. All of the spanners were unexpected, but one that hit especially hard arrived with a thud one busy evening.

It was during the scoring section of a particularly packed quiz night that the gauntlet was laid down. Barry, the self-appointed quiz master, was arguing the toss over whether *Let it Be* or *Abbey Road* was the last album by the Beatles. He wasn't exactly famous for seeing others' point of view, and we had a hard enough time getting him to do things our way in the bar, let alone when we let him loose with a microphone and question sheet. It had taken almost two years of near-constant nagging to persuade Barry that tipping ashtrays in the glass-washing bowl was not a good way to go; nor was it good practice to grab the tea towel used for drying the glasses and mop the sweat off his forehead with it while standing in front of an audience.

As always during the quiz, he was adamantly refusing to admit his error even in the face of blatant facts, diamond-clear logic and a bar full of participants venting their wrath in a hail of ready-salted peanuts.

Joy and I were standing as far apart as possible at either end of the bar, both willing the night to end. We knew that Barry would never give in. Just like he'd refused to accept that safari suits were no longer the height of fashion and that it was no longer deemed socially acceptable, or indeed wise, to openly express an opinion that women were not, and never would be, of equal standing to men.

'Barry! Just keep going,' hissed Joy. 'We're never going to get out of here at this rate.'

She picked a stray peanut out of the pint she was pulling. 'Two hundred and fifty pesetas, please.'

The man handed Joy some coins and took the beer without smiling. I watched as he took a sip and scoured the bar, taking in everything in a slow 360-degree turn.

'Who's that?' I asked.

'No idea.'

Several minutes later, after we'd run the gauntlet of disgruntled quiz teams shuffling out, complaining about how they'd been 'robbed and swindled', the mysterious stranger still sat at the bar nursing the same pint. He had the protruding forehead and facial hair of an animal that had missed the last evolution bus, and a buckled nose that had stopped too many fists.

'Just arrived?' I asked.

'Yeah. This your bar?' he growled back.

'Ours,' I said, nodding towards Joy, who was gathering up beer-sodden quiz papers from the empty tables. 'And my brother's. He's not on tonight.'

'I'm Tel. I've got the bar in the corner.'

'There is no bar,' I said in a tone of voice higher than intended.

'Fackin' will be from next Monday. Your days are numbered, mate.' And with that, he downed half the pint in one gulp, slammed the glass on the bar top and left, but not before holding my gaze for a little longer than you'd call friendly.

Nice, I thought. But that was only the beginning.

Two days later, Tel's Bar had opened amid a jubilee of coloured balloons, luminous chalkboards and menacing scowls. To be truthful, the bar didn't have much going for it from the outset. It was stuck in a corner and the sun rarely shone on its three-table terrace, located directly underneath the footbridge linking the car park to Bar Arancha and the other upper-level *locales*. Inside, the long, narrow bench seats faced the walls like in a railway station waiting room. Little had been done to add charm or character, but still it presented a threat as we envisaged a battle of beer prices ensuing.

During the first few days, a steady trickle of our regulars tried it out, partly out of curiosity, but mostly due to the offer of a free half of beer or glass of wine in the opening week. For most of the time, however, Tel sat pensively, with his feet up on one of his dozen white plastic chairs, sporadically bursting into life as he swatted manically at imaginary flies and glowered at our every move.

At the end of the week, we received our second

visit.

'How much you charging for your drinks?' he barked.

'Why?' asked Joy, folding her arms ready for an argument.

'Cos there's no fackin' point in trying to undercut each other. The only cants that'll win out are the fackin' punters. I'm saying we keep the prices the same. Fack 'em,' he said, nodding his head at a seated family.

And so it was agreed that there would be no war, at least not on the price of drinks. We would compete on a level playing field – albeit one that was already stacked in our favour due to our larger capacity, full programme of entertainment and ten-million-year start on human evolution.

True to his word, Tel did keep his prices on par. We knew because we sent some of our loyal customers on spying missions. And for a while, the healthy disrespect was kept in check, the rules intact. It wouldn't be long until that all changed, however.

~

Now that Steve had slinked off back to Blighty, Joy was noticeably quieter – natural enough, given she was facing yet another life-changing event, though it sparked a sliver of light deep inside my cavernous pit of despair. An air of understanding had crept into her manner towards me. I couldn't tell if it was because her mind was made up and she was beginning her farewell phase, or whether she genuinely felt some sympathy.

Three days before she was due to leave we had our first proper conversation since splitting up. We were on an evening shift and the bar was packed inside and out. The extra help we'd drafted in for our new Saturday Live Band Night were pulling their weight admirably. Well, Danny was. Danny – son of Frank the truck driver – was now sixteen years old, though he was almost as short and skinny as he had been when we'd first accepted his offer of help almost three years earlier. Eager as ever, and always happy to be given something to do, Danny worked harder than any of our other 'adult' helpers. While he rolled a beer barrel in from the stack of twelve we had chained up next to the pool table outside, Sammy was busy plying a quartet of holidaying students with free beer in exchange for cigarettes and banter.

'Alright there, Dan-Dan?' she asked while sitting with the students. 'Just give me a shout, love, if you need a hand.'

'How's the packing going?' I asked Joy, keeping my eyes fixed on Sammy's activities outside.

'Not really started yet,' said Joy. She was chewing on the end of the pink straw protruding from the empty glass she was holding. I'd noticed she'd been drinking more lately.

'I thought you were going Tuesday? Let me know if you need a lift. 'Nother drink?' It was a risky gesture. Would she think I was trying to get rid of her? My head felt she might. Or would she think I was being genuinely considerate – as dictated by my heart.

'Martini and soda,' she said, extending her glass. 'Might have to put it off a week. Steve still has to sort a few things out at his house.'

'Oh.'

'Ask his mum, probably.'

Was that a smirk? A chink in the armour? I passed Joy the drink, holding her gaze. 'Well, like I said, if you need any help...'

She nodded, then brushed a stray strand of fringe from damp brown eyes and looked up, sucking on the straw. 'I'm sorry. I really am.'

'I know,' I said. 'So am I.'

Just then a crowd of people surged through the doors, ready to catch the band. It was all hands on deck.

~

If there's anything that a hotel full of ageing holidaymakers likes to do in the evening, it's to take in a 'good turn'. After much experimentation with cringe-worthy singers and fourth-rate magic acts performing in the asphyxiating confines of our non-air-conditioned bar, we had hit on the idea of hiring a live band to play outside. Not only would they advertise themselves – the sound would carry for miles in the open air – but it had universal appeal and unlike Bingo would not deter the ever-increasing number of non-English-speaking visitors that repopulated the Altamira on a fortnightly basis.

The two-piece band that we employed for the autumn of 1994 proved so popular that the bar was completely full, inside and out. Even 'borrowing' chairs and tables from Bar Arancha after it had closed for the evening wasn't enough to accommodate the crowds that would show up on the Smugglers Tavern Saturday Band Night.

The upper-level overlooking the bar was three-deep with people who were watching entertainment that we were paying a small fortune for. It was decided that Joy should try to extricate a little money from the non-payers upstairs, so while David, Sammy, Danny and I manned the busy bar, off she went with a small silver tray and notepad and pen, taking drinks orders from all and sundry.

Many politely declined, saying they were 'just watching the band', and despite Joy's insistence they continued to stand there happily, grinning and tapping their feet for an hour without contributing a penny. Several did appreciate the waitress service though, including a Russian family of four who insinuated that they did indeed want a drink but only if they could sit down with it.

With a list of drinks orders to pass on, plus our seated patrons to attend to, the pressure was on for Joy to maximise the monetisation of our band night. Having commandeered all the available plastic tables and chairs from Ernesto's upstairs, our seating now extended past the supermarket all the way to a line in the tiles that marked Tel's Bar. I guess to a newly arrived Russian family the terrace looked like a happy community of shared space. Instead of waiting on the stairs while Joy rushed inside to relay their drinks order, they claimed a vacant table at the very back.

Joy emerged from the bar with her silver tray full of beer bottles, tall glasses of exotic mixes and a bottle of Coke with four straws for a family of French timeshare owners who had been shamed into making at least one purchase between them.

After doling out most of the drinks, Joy was left with just those for the Russians, but she couldn't see where the family had gone.

As she looked around, other tables were beckoning her over to place their orders. David and I were also trying to catch her attention to take out the newly poured pints crowding the bar top. John, the singer in the band, was waving an empty glass at her in between lines of 'Love is All Around' by Wet Wet Wet.

Finally she spotted the Russians gesticulating from afar. Weaving her way through the crowd, she hesitated as she approached. They were sitting at one of Tel's tables. To be fair, she did try to cajole them into taking a less contentious position, but they would not be moved and helped themselves to the drinks off the tray before she could stop them. Joy hurried away, hoping Tel hadn't noticed. He had.

At the end of the night, David and I rearranged the chairs and tables on the terrace, returning those that belonged to Ernesto upstairs to Bar Arancha. Joy was about to hose away the cigarette butts and beer stains when Tel bounded up to her like a snarling bulldog, spitting obscenities inches from her face. David and I ran over and, armed with brush and mop, stationed ourselves in front of him.

'Fackin' sort 'er out!' he screamed at David, the only one of us who had managed to maintain diplomatic relations with our noisy neighbour.

'Sort her out?' Joy shouted back. 'I'm not a fucking dog, you twat.' With that, she turned on the hose and doused Tel with a jet of water. Which perhaps wasn't the smartest move.

Tel stepped back for a second, then raised a fist and tried to push past David and me.

'Whoa, back off, pal,' said David.

'Go on, try it, you wet lettuce,' goaded Joy. 'You're all mouth.'

While I coaxed Joy back into the bar, David tried to calm Tel down, but it was too late. As bar owners we'd overstepped the mark. We had served our drinks to people sitting at another bar, then doused the owner when he complained. There was no other way of looking at it except to admit it was a declaration of war.

JOE CAWLEY

CHAPTER TEN

While my dashing bravado with a squeegee mop didn't rekindle any romance between Joy and me, the confrontation with Tel did reignite a sense of camaraderie, helping to defrost the chilly atmosphere that had prevailed for the last few weeks. This, coupled with the confirmation that Joy had postponed her exit for yet 'another week or so', added a little spring to my step that couldn't be contained even in the face of the vitriol that was being hurled on a daily basis from Tel's Bar.

Every promotion that we highlighted in bright chalk on the blackboard at the top of the steps was copied and taken one step further by Tel. If we had Karaoke, he had Karaoke *plus* Bingo the same night. If we had Roast Lamb Special, he had Roast Lamb Special *and* a free glass of wine. The gauntlet really was down. Even some of our most loyal patrons were deserting us as Tel won them over with free drinks and special discounts.

The lightening of Joy's mood took me completely by surprise and I began to allow myself to think about the possibility of us getting back together. However, she was still adamant that she was leaving Tenerife and going to live with Steve and that a call from England was imminent.

Although that particular call was a long time coming, the phone was never silent for long. The lure of a sunny beach resort meant that everybody and his donkey were now phoning to say 'Long time no see... when can we come over and stay in your apartment to have a free holiday'. Okay, maybe not in quite such a direct fashion, but it was certainly the objective for many of them. Long-lost nephews, aunties, and cousins three times removed had decided that chez Joe and Joy was now a ready-made, all-inclusive, fully serviced holiday apartment available 365 days a year absolutely free. Damn! If I hadn't moved there myself, *I'd* have befriended me pretty darn quick.

Of course real family and friends had always been welcome when Joy and I were together, so long as they realised that just because they were on holiday, it didn't mean we were too. We had little enough leisure as it was, so when we did have guests, we had to schedule our time with them very carefully. Most were also more than willing to help out, either in the bar or on the domestic front. In fact anybody that offered to help was most welcome, even more so if they weren't staying with us too.

One family member that did take us by surprise with her offer of help was Nan, though how much help an eighty-five-year-old could offer was open to debate. Nan had been a huge influence in both my life and David's, always happy to see us and providing a warm, loving refuge when our parents went on holiday or needed a break from two scrapping infants.

It's funny how certain senses can spark a nostalgic memory. In one or two British bars in Tenerife the perennial smell of corned beef stew and pickled onions, and the unmistakable whiff of stale urine that doggedly clings to the fibres of all senior citizens' toilet rugs would always whisk me back to my Nan's house in Clitheroe.

Which is exactly where I was heading on my first visit to the UK since moving away three years earlier. It had been decided by proxy that I was to go to Blighty to bring Nan back to Tenerife now that we were in a post-summer October lull. I'd like to think I was chosen because, out of David, Joy and me, I was the most compassionate and responsible. But that wasn't the case. I knew really that I was the most dispensable, Joy being the face that everybody came to see, and David being a far better cook. Joy had agreed that, even if Steve called, she would not leave the bar understaffed and return to England until after I got back.

At Reina Sofia Airport I sat contemplating the fact that I was returning to England as a non-resident, a foreigner almost. It felt a little odd but also exhilarating. Being free of the shackles of everyday life and labour in the UK meant that I could appreciate it through the eyes of a visitor and I was curious as to how that would seem.

I wanted to forget the conventions, be ignorant of the rules. I could use the excuse of 'I don't live here' if anybody questioned my behaviour. The anticipation was the same as when I had worked with a temp agency. I had requested that I was only assigned short contracts of no longer than a week. I enjoyed stepping into other people's lives, taking a fleeting glance at their day-to-day activities without becoming involved. It was try-before-you-buy lifestyle shopping. Perhaps I was still window-shopping even now with the Smugglers Tavern. Maybe my money would forever stay in my pocket, that ultimate lifestyle purchase never made.

Curiously, this was exactly how I shopped for

anything. Even as a toddler, with my 25p pocket money clenched in a tiny fist, I would insist on looking at every shelf in every toyshop before making a decision, wary of missing out on anything. It would secretly infuriate Mum but she rarely made a fuss, opting to allow me the independence of choice. Permanence frightened me even then. As a fully subscribed opportunist I felt compelled to try anything new that came my way – as long as it didn't mean that I had to stick with it.

There was a certain amount of satisfaction in the fact that Joy, David and I had already served three summers at the Smugglers Tavern. Most of those months had been successful, success being a relative term. On a business level, we hadn't poisoned too many people; and our sanity had remained pretty much intact, save for the odd hour of babbling, bog-eyed consciousness – usually while waiting for the last drinkers to empty their glasses and stagger back to their snug beds, leaving us to mop the sticky floor tiles, prise diced carrot from the urinals and change those tablecloths that our junior patrons had blown snotty noses on.

On a personal level, we'd already lost one partner – Faith having decided that her fear of matches, zero stress tolerance and general allergy to people meant that she was not best suited to a career in the hospitality trade. Now, like the Smugglers' interior upholstery, the remaining relationship had become a little threadbare to say the least.

On the fraternal front, although the brotherly love had resurfaced thanks to Joy's affair, in general the interaction between David and me extended no further than cursing each other if I burnt the chips or he set fire to the tea towels again. As is probably the case with most brothers, we were never outwardly close, though our strong emotional bond ensured that when push came to shove we were always there for each other.

However, recently it had been ourselves who had been doing the pushing and shoving as the frustration and boredom of our day-in, day-out routine started to get the better of us. It only took one condiment set to have not been filled by the other for the sniping to begin.

'Salt's empty.'

'And?'

'S'pose I'll have to do it again then.'

'I guess.'

'Dickhead.'

'Twat.'

'Is that gammon with egg or pineapple?'

'Egg.'

'Knob.'

~

The plane was going to be late – 'air-traffic congestion', apparently; one of many modern excuses bandied around in nasal tones by today's airport announcers. Honesty seems to be a policy of the past when it comes to public travel announcements, where fuzzy fob-offs are the order of the day. 'A confused customer is easier to deal with than an informed one' reads the public relations training manual. Ambivalent reasons such as 'the plane's gone tech', or 'there's been a passenger allocation download' are applied to all manner of delays, even when it might be no more than a simple case of deliberate overbooking or drunken ground crew biffing the planes with motorised stepladders.

I now had two hours to kill so I sat down with a coffee and yesterday's news. Whilst browsing through the page-three exploits of our future king, I sensed the man sitting next to me was reading page two. I was not amused. Reading, in whatever form, should be a private luxury, enjoyed without haste or disruption and not part of a team effort.

'Would you like the paper when I've finished?' I asked, peering over Prince Charles.

'No, no. You're alright, I just want to read that piece on interest rates,' he replied.

He continued to lean in, squinting, which left me in a bit of a dilemma. Did I wait for him to finish before I turned the page or make a stand and ignore him. Being British and therefore completely incapable of such affront, I found myself holding the newspaper open for him while I gazed around the airport terminal.

'Okay, turn over,' he said after a couple of minutes. I found myself complying and dutifully turned the next page. 'Okay, turn over,' he repeated after a quick scan. 'Nope, nothing there either. Next page.' He tutted. 'I don't know why you buy the *Daily Mail*, there's nothing in it. Get a decent paper next time, eh, mate?' And off he trotted, leaving me still holding the paper up.

I tossed it into a bin and wandered off to see how else I could amuse myself. There are few places better suited to people-watching than airport terminals. A whole host of characters pass through these places, providing a never-ending supply of business travellers, frequent flyers, and – the most entertaining to watch – bewildered tourists.

A traffic jam of trolleys was piling up in one of the entrances as a silver-haired man sporting an olive-green safari suit and yellow cravat squinted at the information board. The sliding doors gave up trying to decide if people were coming or going and settled on bad-tempered snapping like a blood-frenzied shark. Reacting to the irate shouts, the man shuffled out of the way, allowing the masses to pour in around him.

Even though it was only ten in the morning, tracksuited holidaymakers surrounded the bar, wringing their last holiday moments from plastic cups of beer. One particularly sunburned individual was loudly trying to order a bag of crisps, but the man behind the bar couldn't decipher his strong Geordie accent. 'Crisps, mon! Y'know, chiz 'n' onion, like?'

I carried on walking, although in truth every fifth step counted as a skip as I was repeatedly bitten on the heel by a trolley whose distracted handlers were trying to round up a herd of children. 'Rebecca! Ger 'ere now!' they shouted as Rebecca led her three younger siblings on a campaign of terror, nipping the legs of oncoming travellers. I was rammed once more as the crowd in front came to a sudden halt. Up ahead, the man in the cravat was standing mid-stream, squinting at another information board and looking even more perplexed.

'What flight are you looking for?' I asked.

'I don't know,' he replied still peering at the

screen. 'I'm supposed to be going back to Luton today, but I can't see any Luton flights on the board.'

He passed me his ticket and I immediately spotted his problem. 'You're a bit early, mate. The flight doesn't go till tomorrow,' I informed him, showing him the date.

'But it says Monday, 10.45... Look.'

'That's your flight number – MON 1045 – Monarch, flight one-zero-four-five. You might as well go and have another day on the beach.'

Without a word, he wandered out of the airport for an unexpected extension to his stay.

Sometimes, travel staff don't need to follow a policy of client confusion, customers are quite capable of causing it themselves.

I usually don't like to get involved in early conversation with my seat neighbours. You just don't know what nutter is going to demand your attention for the ensuing four hours. I prefer easing my conscience with a polite remark as the airplane's wheels hit the tarmac, safe in the knowledge that escape is only minutes away. Sometimes though, there's no choice.

'Not much of a tan there, have you?' The man beside me was glowing like a radioactive beacon with blisters.

I considered my options: a) smile, nod and feign intense concentration as I study the instructions on the sick bag, b) acknowledge my pallor and reveal a dislike of the outdoors, c) admit that I live in Tenerife. The last option I knew to be particularly hazardous, having suffered the predictable interrogation many times – 'Do you live there? Do you like it? How long have you—' Blah blah blah.

I reached for the sick bag.

'Now that's a tan,' he said. Splashes of beer leapt onto my lap from a can of Carling Black Label as a scorched arm was extended in my face. 'Trouble is, it never lasts. Two days after I've got home it's all peeled off.' I could see his problem. A piece of arm skin dangled precariously over my Jack Daniels and Coke.

I'd finished reading the sick bag and moved on to testing the food tray, flipping it up and down a few times, but it was no use, the beacon wanted to enthuse.

'I love Tenerife, don't you? I've been coming three times a year for the last ten years. Betty here...' He poked a stumpy thumb towards a velour-suited lady, who screwed her whole face into a smile. Under a tangle of blonde tints and silver roots she looked like a discarded Christmas decoration.

'HELLO,' she shouted, fumbling to find the armrest volume switch.

'She says she doesn't know what we'd do if we didn't get away from it all now and then.'

I carried on nodding while trying to avoid eye contact lest it suggest that I was interested. Rummaging in the seat back, I pulled out a dog-eared in-flight magazine and flicked idly through the articles on celebrity greenhouses and ten things not to miss if I ever visit Bratislava in Slovakia – the return flight was the first thing that sprang to mind.

The man beside me continued. 'We always stay in the same hotel, right in the thick of it. We get breakfast, lunch and dinner in Union Jack's next door. D'you know it? Brilliant food! Holland's pies, real English bacon, none of that foreign stuff – you know what you're getting. Know what I mean?'

'Have you ever tried Spanish food?' I asked calmly.

'Nah. Why would I? I know what I like and I like what I know.'

I decided there was no point in continuing the discussion, but he decided otherwise.

'They've got proper English beer for a pound a pint. For less than a tenner I get kegged every afternoon. And the videos... Now, come on, you've got to admit that Jeremy Beadle's funny, I mean, I could watch him all day.' He paused for a moment, reflecting on his 'foreign holiday', adding contemplatively, 'In fact, I did watch him all day yesterday.'

I quietly sighed at the thought of how many people go abroad without really leaving home, seeking solace in familiarity, afraid to venture beyond the sensory walls they've built up through years of insularity. It just seemed such a waste. The irony was that we were the suppliers in this improper trade. We'd tried offering tapas, tried to point people in the direction of Canarian restaurants and bars and suggested patches of the real Tenerife for a day out, but sadly there were few takers.

'You can keep England for me. I think I might move abroad one day,' I heard my seat neighbour say before I plugged in my earphones. I seriously doubted he knew where abroad actually was.

Four hours later we landed in 'abroad', but this abroad looked gloomy and dismal, sucked dry of all colour. What had happened to the quintessential chocolate-box image of England as portrayed in gentle murder mysteries on daytime TV?

Still, there was always Clitheroe, a bastion of twee-ness boasting sun-filled beer gardens, manicured cricket lawns and ice-cream vans selling the same frozen, sugary goods that have stickied the fingers of children since the 1950s. Or at least that was how I remembered it looking on that June day in 1991 when I said goodbye to Nan before we originally left for Tenerife.

CHAPTER ELEVEN

The flight delay meant that I'd missed the last train to central Manchester so I had to take a bus. It was closing time for the pubs and I could feel tension in the air.

As we passed through Wythenshawe, a shoe-less boy sat on the ground under a dilapidated bus shelter, pointing and laughing out loud at the traffic. He couldn't have been more than twelve years old but his face showed signs of having seen too much already. Further down the road, a rock was thrown, startling me and the only other passenger on the bus at that point. Frail and nervy, the lady was deep into her pension years. She was bundled in several layers of fading woollens, topped with a clear plastic rain hood. The driver fleetingly glanced in his mirror as the rock bounced off the back of the bus. Two young boys gave chase, trying to jump onto the moving vehicle.

The main shopping area of Sharston was boarded up, scrawled signatures on the walls of the job centre reminding anybody who cared to notice that they 'were here on 20/10/91'. Through the rain-streaked windows of the Jolly Carter I could see two skinheads playing pool, the rest of the lounge deserted.

A trio with melancholic faces boarded at the next stop, careful not to make eye contact. Behind them a drunk struggled to find forward gear, then managed to winch himself up by the handrail. He spilled the correct money onto the driver's tray.

'How you doing, Jim?' the driver sighed.

''Ave 'ad a bit to drink tonight,' he slurred.

'Aye, I can see that. Go on then.' He nodded to the back of the bus. 'And don't piss on the seats this time.'

Jim struggled up the bus, trying to judge when his feet were going to make contact with the floor. 'He's alright, 'im. He's a good mate, he is,' he announced to the other passengers before falling into the luggage compartment and commencing a very loud sleep.

Northenden was a model of mixed cultures. Chinese, Indian, Chinese, Indian, Chinese, Italian, Indian, chippy. Nice to see that our great British cuisine was holding its own in an area of so many other exotic temptations.

A boy in last season's Manchester United kit boarded, his face covered in mud and despondency. Had he lost a match or was this just still Northenden?

The lights grew marginally brighter as we passed along Palatine Road into Didsbury. Here the houses were grander. Victorian bedsits and guest houses for the goth-costumed students, who could be seen laughing inside the Four In Hand pub, exchanging grant cheques for pints of lager and lime. They were temporary revellers at a party for the poor, whose impoverished hosts resented their freedom to leave when that final bell rang.

Down Wilmslow Road into Withington the streets grew wider and the choice of eateries even more varied. Italian, Indian, Mexican, American, Turkish and Greek, side by side, neon red and fluorescent yellow vying for the hungry. Fallowfield, however, invited no lingering. The flashing blue alarm over Pandora's Sauna warned people to move on once they'd got their food from Abdul's, or Hajji's Take-Out.

Across Platt Bridge, the variety of accents on the bus broadened as we passed by the many curry houses of Rusholme and fashion shops such as Bombay Looks, selling the latest in saris. Student town was upon us again. Fly posters on every available surface clamoured for a piece of student loan.

At Chorlton Street Bus Station I ignored the unsavoury suggestions from a trio of pasty hookers waiting for clients. For the price of a round of Boddingtons they offered instant gratification behind the peeling advertising hoarding. 'Smoking Can Kill' said the small print in 12-inch lettering. So could sharing your fluids with a toothless sixty-year-old, I thought as I strode past a gum-chewing grandmother dressed in a pink plastic mini-skirt.

I struggled to read the Perspex timetable as it was covered in permanent marker. A driver was sitting behind the wheel of the nearest bus, reading *The Sun*.

'Where does the next bus to Clitheroe leave from?' I asked.

'Over there, mate,' he said, pointing. 'But not till tomorrow.'

'I thought there was one tonight at twelve?'

'There was, but you just missed him. He always leaves early so he can get home and shag the babysitter before his missus gets back from bingo.'

The driver's dedication to extracurricular activities meant that I had come 2,000 miles only to face the prospect of sleeping in a rapidly emptying bus station with half a dozen ladies of the night and a drugged-up overcoat who was debating the merits of self-image with a vending machine. 'Am a fuckin' shithead,' he remonstrated, pointing a finger at a solitary Kit Kat, the last remaining resident in the confectionary tower-block. 'What the fuck did you do that for anyways, you twat? Don't you call me a twat, ya twat... Ah fuck off... No, youse fuck off... No, youse fuck off.'

'Where you goin', man? Clitheroe? I'll take you for fifty quid.'

I wheeled round to face a hooded youth hopping from foot to foot. His eyes had the shine of brand-new double-glazing.

'I'm not paying fifty quid to get to Clitheroe.' Certainly not with a stoned white rapper, I thought but didn't add.

'Twenny-five then, bruv,' he offered, still hopping.

My choices were, without doubt, extremely limited. I decided to take my chances with the spliff-toting taxi driver, and he led me to a side street where my limousine awaited.

'You'll 'ave to get in my side, that door's bollocksed.'

I clambered into the fragrant orange ruins of what was once a Datsun Cherry, careful not to put my foot through the hole in the floor, as instructed.

After several false starts he managed to wrench some life out of the engine and we set off accompanied by the booming sounds of the Stone Roses. I was getting tired and what with the stinging fumes of a newly lit joint, my eyes begged to close, but my companion was seeing the world as he'd never seen it before and wanted to share it all with me.

'Look at that city, man. Those lights. Is that sweet or what? Now tell me that scene means nothin' to yer.'

It did mean something to me, namely a life left behind, a life that had been in limbo, shuffling sideways without purpose or direction. I knew that behind the bricks, the glass, the plasterboard walls there were many in the same boat, certain that there had to be more to life than drifting aimlessly for decades, until that all-illuminating moment in the armchair when, greyed and slippered, it would suddenly dawn that it was just too damn late. All the infinite dreams of youth, desires of adulthood and great plans for middle age would now remain unfulfilled and the only thing to look forward to was a quiet and peaceful death.

Remarkably we got to Clitheroe without major incident. My lungs had suffered and my head was somewhat light, not unpleasantly though. I paid him and waved as he drove off, backfiring a farewell and trailing a cloud of illicit fumes all the way down Whalley Road. Bed beckoned.

I knocked and let myself in. I'd told Nan that she should keep the front door locked but she argued that nobody would be able to get in if she did.

The tiny living room was cluttered with odds and ends. Ceramic funfair prizes were displayed alongside Jubilee mugs and postcards in a precariously leaning glass cabinet. Above the electric fire a collection of teaspoons shared wall-space with photographs of my brother, my late dad and me.

Nan was asleep in the armchair. A large magnifying glass rested on top of the *Daily Express* folded in her lap. The sideboard stereo by her side was swamped in old newspapers, boiled-sweet wrappers and an assortment of pens. On a side table to her left sat a mug of cold Horlicks topped with a thin, wrinkly skin and a plate of shortbread biscuits that I assumed had either been left out for me or any passing burglar.

The hairdresser must have been today. Her thin white hair was puffed like a dandelion head about to blow off in the wind. I didn't want to startle her so I stage-whispered 'Nan' from the doorway.

Slowly her eyes flickered to life and a short smile followed a pause for recognition.

'Must've dropped off,' she said slowly.

'How you doing?' I bent down to kiss her tissue-thin cheeks. For eighty-five she looked remarkably well. Her insistence that she was related to the Queen meant she was resolute in keeping up appearances. Rarely would Nan be seen without her Barbara Cartland face and string of pearls.

Upstairs, the bed creaked as I pulled a bobbled winceyette sheet, a ribbed blanket, a 4-inch quilt, a tartan top blanket and a floral bedspread over me. After thirty seconds I thrust them all back, turned off the electric blanket and tossed the hot water bottle onto the threadbare carpet.

As I lay there I pictured Joy serving pint after pint, making idle chat with the barflies and generally stuck in a Groundhog Day loop of endless smiles and inane banter with 'pleased to see you' tattooed on her face. I wondered if she'd given me a second

100

thought, if she missed me at all. God, I missed her, despite all that had gone on.

Early the following morning I relieved Nan's fridge of all things inedible before she woke. One of Mr Kipling's apple pies had grown exceedingly hazardous and a chipped jug of milk had crusted over. 'Waste not, want not,' she would counter whenever I'd confronted her with a pot of yoghurt or tin of mandarin slices whose sell-by date signalled an era gone by. Still, she'd amassed a commendable number of years and although her legs were swollen and reluctant to move, she was nonetheless in remarkable health.

Nan asked me to go to the bank with her. 'Put a suit and tie on,' she insisted, 'the manager might see us.'

I politely declined to wear my dead granddad's safari suit, but before I had time to object to a tie as well, she'd lassoed me with a particularly gaudy kipper model from the musty suitcase that housed a few of her late husband's belongings.

I scratched at a scab camouflaged in the paisley pattern. 'It's got mushy peas on it,' I said, as she stood on the settee pushing the knot of the tie deep into my Adam's apple.

'And here, I found this.' She held out a plastic jar of Brylcreem. 'Sort your hair out, you look like a scarecrow.'

We entered the bank in Clitheroe town centre with Nan dressed like Eliza Doolittle in *My Fair Lady* and me still tugging at the 6-inch-wide paisley boa constrictor squeezing my neck and dangling in front of my crotch. For an old lady, she could still tie a mean knot.

I held Nan's arm as we stepped forward to the counter. 'I'd like to buy some Spanish potatoes, thank you,' she said in her best BBC voice.

'Pesetas,' I explained to the blank face behind the counter.

'Ah. Just a minute,' said the bank clerk. 'Mrs Kenyon, isn't it?'

'Yes,' hissed Nan, her teeth gritted in a frozen smile.

'I think the bank manager would like a word, if you don't mind waiting a minute.'

Nan dug her elbow into my ribs. 'See, aren't you glad you put your tie on now?' she whispered through her teeth.

One of the oak panels in the wall to the side of us creaked open and a tall, balding man beckoned us into his office. He helped Nan into a chair, where she sat bolt upright, nodding politely as he spent several minutes explaining in simple terms that her savings would be much better off in a different kind of account. 'So would that be alright, Mrs Kenyon?' he concluded. He leaned in and raised his eyebrows, smiling as he waited for her agreement.

Nan looked up at me out of the corner of her eye. 'What did he say?'

I repeated the gist of what the bank manager had explained. 'Sounds good to me, Nan. Is that okay with you?'

'Splendid,' she said brightly, and stood up, rummaging in her handbag as the manager held the door open for us.

'Thank-you for your time, you've been most helpful,' she said. 'This is for you.' And she placed a fifty-pence piece in his outstretched palm.

~

After dropping Nan back home, I wrestled off the tie and headed out to revisit Bolton market. This was partly to stock up on some potted shrimps for Nan ('for the journey'), but also because I was curious to see how I would feel back at the starting point of our overseas adventure. I wanted to see if I could recapture some of the excitement of how it felt standing among the shuffling shoppers knowing that I would soon be jetting off to a foreign land. Perhaps it would help me appreciate that the grass actually was greener on the other side.

Nothing had changed in Bolton, including the weather. It was just over three years since Joy and I had filleted our last fish and pushed out three trays of chicken legs for a fiver. Six months we had worked there, enduring the early mornings, freezing weather and stinking conditions. Most of the time I had hated it, but it was now a part of my history, a particular low in my working life without which I wouldn't have been so tempted to make such a humongous change.

I took a deep breath and stepped from the rain through a gap in the market's huge metal doors. Outside, everybody had been trudging head down, faces tight and dripping with rain, eyes on the pavement, avoiding shoe-drowning puddles. Inside, there was an altogether chirpier atmosphere. Under the bright yellow flicker of artificial lighting, white-coated stallholders hurled banter at each other across a cortege of anorak hoods and plastic rain bonnets shuffling between the produce.

'Hey, Jim. How's the rash?'

'Lorraine, call that a flash? Make an old man happy, show us a proper flash.'

'Stevie, you been taking the ugly tablets again?'

Pat was the instigator of much of the abuse, his ruddy cheeks like red flares in the sea of white coats, grey fish and thin plastic parsley dividers. When abuse wasn't being hurled across the aisles, it was rained down on his own employees in a stream of remonstrations for not shouting the odds loud enough, not working hard enough and generally just for being there. If he got bored of insulting his workers, the spotlight was turned onto his customers. Most took it in good spirits, some didn't and would never be seen there again. Deterring custom didn't seem to be an issue for Pat; he considered it all part of being a stallholder, right up there with refreezing the stock as many times as he could get away with and trying to dupe the suppliers any which way he could. Anybody was game for abuse in Pat's eyes; we'd all had our fair share over the years, including Joy and me.

Joy could give as much back, quick with the retorts and completely immune to any personal insult. I guess I was of a more sensitive nature and preferred to just keep my head down in the hope that the venomous arrows would land elsewhere.

I thoroughly expected to feel the wrath as I approached the stall, but instead, a beam stretched across Pat's chubby face.

'Jeffin' hell. The wanderer returns! Missed us too much, eh?'

'Not a lot. Back in Blighty for a few days, so just

thought I'd say hello. How's trade?'

'Oh, you know. Never enough.' He shrugged. 'Mind, never jeffin' will be with this motley bunch of tossers. Useless, the lot of 'em. Come round and say hello.'

I ducked under a trio of sea bass and emerged on the business side of the stall. Nothing had changed. Styrofoam boxes lay scattered and broken under the stalls, cardboard boxes of chicken thighs were stacked along a length of splintered pallets behind the workers and an assortment of greying fish and chicken innards were splattered on the metal framework like huge discarded bogeys.

As I was saying hello to the old and new faces I spotted Duncan stomping through the crowd of shoppers, lips gurning and eyebrows dancing up and down as he barged everyone out of the way.

'Fook! Doe! Where you been? Where Doy?' he said, reaching across the stall to give me a hug. Poking from the same blue snorkel jacket I remembered from years ago, his newly shaved head looked like a broken bowling ball. A wide scar zigzagged from forehead to right ear, his right eye purple from what I presumed was yet another beating from the local skinheads.

'You've missed your girlfriend, haven't you, Duncan?' said Seafood Sandra.

'Fook off,' said Duncan, raising two fingers.

'Hey, Duncan, isn't that your mam?' said Mac, pointing.

As Duncan turned round, Mac gently put a rabbit's head in his hood.

'Ten points, Mac lad,' said Pat, smiling.

Yep, nothing had changed. Life on the market

continued as it always had. I watched an enraged Duncan spin round like a dog chasing his tail, elbow in the air as he tried to remove the rabbit.

'Is this fresh today, love?' A bony finger was prodding a fillet of hake.

A cold flush signalled it was time for me to move on. It was as if I was afraid that if I stayed behind the stall, Tenerife might never really have happened, turning out to be just a ludicrous dream from which I was now awakening.

As I said my farewells, turned up my collar and marched head down into the rain of Ashburner Street I felt a surge of longing, for blue skies and tropical landscapes, for sunshine on my back and an ocean breeze on my face. I couldn't wait to get back.

~

Back in Clitheroe, Nan was busy in the kitchen, steam rising from two saucepans of tinned new potatoes and tinned carrots.

The kitchen table had been laid for two, which was unusual as Nan usually took herself off into the front room while guests ate. Two plates of meat and potato pie with boiled potatoes and carrots were placed on the plastic green tablecloth. The centre of the table was busy with stubby stainless steel salt- and pepper shakers, a jug of piping-hot gravy and a small glass bowl of pickled onions, an obligatory addition to every meal at Nan's.

As she sat down, I could tell Nan was preoccupied.

'Help yourself to ketchup,' she said, pointing a

knife at the gravy. 'So…' she continued, then didn't.

'You okay, Nan?' I said quietly.

She took her time to answer, rolling a pickled onion around her mouth like a cow chewing grass.

'What's it like… Tenerife?' she said, without looking up.

'Well, it's—'

'I've never been, see.'

'No, I, erm… I think you'll like it.'

Nan put down her knife and fork and cleared both our plates, despite me having only taken a couple of mouthfuls.

'Good. That's settled then.'

I waited for a little more explanation but none was forthcoming.

'What's settled?'

'I'm coming with you back to Tenerife. Apple pie?' she said, offering a bowl of pickled onions.

'I know, that's why I'm here, to take you back.'

She paused while the thought registered. 'Oh. I'll get my coat then, shall I?'

JOE CAWLEY

CHAPTER TWELVE

Two short toots of the horn broke the nervous silence.

'He's here, Nan!' I shouted.

She sat opposite, clutching an enormous cream handbag to her disproportionately small body.

'Is he here?' she said, after clacking her teeth back into place with her tongue.

I opened the door and an icy blast of October morning swept in from the phosphorous-yellow street. There was silence except for the low murmur of the taxi ticking over to keep the heater on inside.

'Mornin',' said a chirpy pensioner, rubbing his tan driving gloves together. It was partly to keep warm and partly in excitement at the prospect of a trip to Manchester Airport.

Clitheroe is a postage-stamp continent. Many of its residents are the descendants of generations that have grown up under the rueful gaze of Pendle Hill, home of the infamous Pendle Witches. Whether due to some medieval curse or just a simple lack of inclination, it seems that many people born in Clitheroe just never leave. Ever. Not even for a holiday. It's a champion of parochialism, an icon of insularity.

During a previous stay with my nan while I was still a UK resident, I had risked a visit to the local hairdresser's. In pursuit of polite conversation, the stylist asked where I was from. She obviously knew that I was an out-of-towner as my clothes were from neither Jessop's outfitters on Brownlow Lane, nor the younger and more daring Style Palace, shameful purveyors of short skirts – 'short' in Clitheroe describing any garment that revealed anything more than a teasing glimpse of upper shin.

'Manchester,' I replied, eliciting a little shriek of delight from the teenager.

'Oooh, Manchester? I'd love to go to Manchester, me!'

Her eyes glazed over and she was gone, scissors held high, dreaming of the mysterious wonders that Manchester must hold, all of 30 miles away.

You can tell how self-absorbed a village is by reading the local newspaper. In a sleepy village like Clitheroe, real newsworthy events rarely occur. Undeterred by this, the local paper continues to fill its pages with such interesting stories as 'Butcher Gets New Sign', accompanying this with a photo of a proud butcher standing outside Broadbottoms the Butcher's, imaginatively captioned, 'Charles with his new sign outside Broadbottoms the Butcher's'.

Nan once received a pair of people-shaped slippers from my dad, who was living in America at the time. A local reporter heard about her transatlantic footwear and sure enough a proud Nan in said slippers graced the front page of the very next edition. Disappointingly, she had to retire them from use as the left ear of the right slipper kept catching on the right ear of the left slipper. More than once Nan had been seen through her little front room window suddenly bursting into a spontaneous quickstep as the ears interlocked.

The slippers were coming with us, however, as Nan had developed a fondness for 'the twins', as she called them. Those slippers were pampered like a family pet. They had their own place on the front

110

room windowsill, next to a framed photo of an old man laughing in the rain. We had all thought he was a long-lost relative or a secret lover of old, until the same framed image was spotted by David wrapped in cellophane on the shelves of several branches of WH Smith.

Nan had veered from one extreme to the other in her packing. I had retrieved the biggest suitcase I could find from the back of a musty bedding cupboard and then left her for a few hours while I went into the town centre to cancel milk, papers and her subscriptions to *Knitting Weekly* and *Extreme Snowboarding*. When I came back she announced that she'd done the packing. On closer inspection her preparations were a little lacking. The only items she'd put in the suitcase were seven pairs of underpants, a straw hat, one pair of shoes comprising two incompatible individuals, and 'the twins', along with a collection of household items that she thought might come in useful.

'Nan, I think you may need more clothes than this,' I reminded her, as I removed a teapot, the television remote control ('I don't want to miss *Coronation Street*') and a woolly toilet roll holder that she had knitted for herself many years before her fingers had become arched with arthritis.

A few white lies had been necessary to overcome Nan's anxiety about flying. I informed her that she would only be in the air for a few minutes and that, much to her relief, she wouldn't miss *Corrie* as there were televisions on the plane. Thus deceived, albeit kindly, she agreed to go, but with a warning that if it was too hot she'd be on the next bus home.

~

The driver attempted to lift Nan's case himself but it was futile. In a pique of child-like stubbornness she had insisted on packing her entire collection of funfair-prize ornaments and cushioned coat hangers. Between us we eventually managed to hoist the case into the boot of the shiny, and now rearing, Austin Allegro.

'Come on, Nan.' I offered an arm and led her to the taxi.

'Where's me handbag?' she panicked, wheeling round with both hands firmly clasped around the object of her anxiety.

'You're holding it, Nan.'

'Well. I'll go to the foot of our stairs! Silly bugger,' she said, shaking her head.

Her handbag was her life-support machine. Within its deep recesses lay absolutely everything that she, or whoever she happened to be within tottering assistance of, could possibly need. Not once had that handbag let her down. It was a department store of essential items. Third floor, Ladies Accessories – scented tissues, scarlet lipsticks, snowy-white powder puffs; second floor, Refreshments – barley sugars, mint imperials, old bits of chicken wrapped in foil ('waste not, want not'); first floor, Medicinal Items – angina pills, wrinkle potions, corn plasters; ground floor, Assorted Miscellany – Daniel O'Donnell cassette, large-print Mills & Boon, large tin of buttons, small tin of safety pins.

As we drove along the deserted roads, for the first time since stepping foot back on Blighty, I felt envious of the people in their huddled terraced houses, snug and comfortable in the knowledge that in the morning they would get up at the same time as yesterday, go through the same dressing and breakfast rituals and set off for their regular work to meet familiar faces.

The thought gave me a jolt. Security, cosy comforts and routine were the very things I'd been glad to get away from in Tenerife. Now they were the very things that I yearned for, since splitting up with Joy.

Even though it was the early hours of the morning, the airport was humming with activity. Excited holidaymakers in Adidas and Reebok mingled with impassive businessmen of various nationalities.

'Look at all those darkies!' shrieked Nan, grabbing hold of my wrist. A vibrant clan in multi-coloured robes illuminated the melee at the Air Zimbabwe check-in desk. She couldn't take her eyes off them as we forced our complaining trolley into line behind the extensive stretch of people keen to begin their holiday.

When our time came, we were asked all the routine questions about whether we had packed ourselves, had anybody tampered with our cases, did we have any electrical goods, and so on. Nan did what she always does in unfamiliar situations and began to rummage in her bag.

'Where are we?' she asked, elbow-deep in exploration.

'We're at the check-in, Nan,' I explained.

'Oh. Here then, let me get it,' she insisted, extending a handful of loose change to the check-in girl.

'No. Check-in, not checkout,' I explained, curling her fingers back over the assortment of coins, buttons and tablets.

I was in desperate need of the toilet and so in the main departure lounge I left Nan sitting down with the trolley, under strict instructions not to move. I slowly backed away, finger raised as though training a dog. Needless to say, when I returned, the trolley had obeyed but Nan hadn't.

In my absence she had noticed that the well-to-do lady facing her was sipping on a cup of tea she had brought down from the self-service cafeteria overlooking the main lounge area. Unhappy that the lady hadn't asked if she wanted one, Nan put on a show of huffing, tutting loudly and repeatedly turning her cheek. Uncomfortable, yet completely unaware of her social faux pas, the lady had gathered up her mohair overcoat and Gucci accessories and retreated to find an area where drinking tea was not considered so offensive. Nan then decided to get one for herself. Eventually, after a succession of trips up and down the escalator, she found the cafeteria, helped herself to a cup of tea and took it straight to a table, oblivious to the ''Scuse me, love,' from the till girl, whose scant training probably hadn't included a section on dealing with delinquent pensioners who don't pay.

'Have you seen a little old lady in a beige overcoat and black furry hat?' I asked everybody seated near the orphaned trolley.

A young girl pointed upwards. I followed her aim to the restaurant area on the next level.

'You okay, Nan?' I said softly, relieved at having

found her relatively easily.

The electrical impulses in her head halted their random careering, banging into each other as they did, then begrudgingly fell into an orderly line to deliver a message of recognition.

'Oh. Hello, love. Fancy seeing you here! Would you like a cup of tea? I've just made some.'

At the departure gate we commandeered a wheelchair that was forlornly staring at the wall. As invalids, infants and the infirm are always boarded first, I saw this as an express route through.

'Jump in and look ill,' I said to Nan, who stealthily climbed aboard and then proceeded to dramatically clutch her stomach and howl like a demented wolf. Twenty-five years of am-dram at Clitheroe Operatic Society had clearly not been wasted.

'Not that ill,' I hissed, 'or they won't let us on.'

Nan resorted to silent wincing at anybody that cared to look, which after her previous performance included just about everybody.

We did indeed get to go on first and were strapped into our seats along with the other, presumably genuine, wheelchair jockeys before the plane filled up with able-bodied passengers. Nan began to fidget again in this unfamiliar environment. She unlocked the seat tray and pulled it down hard a few times to test its strength, causing the old man in front to bob up and down like a duck in water. She flicked the light on and off, called the stewardess a few times for good measure and then disappeared backwards as exploring fingers discovered the seat recline button. There she stayed for a few moments, studying the signs on the plastic overhead compartment.

'Why do I have a life-jacket under my seat?'

'Because we fly over water.'

'Will I need to put it on then?'

'No. Only if we have to make an emergency landing at sea.'

'But I've got me best shoes on.'

She thankfully spent the entire journey flicking through the channels of the in-flight entertainment and when we touched down at Reina Sofia was a little surprised to learn that we had even taken off.

I spent most of the flight absently gazing out of the windows at the sea of clouds below. Although the anger and hurt remained, those emotions were being smothered by an overwhelming sense of excitement at the prospect of life getting back to how it used to be. It had become clear that my love for Joy was still there; it had been tainted by her deception, but it was a love worth fighting for. She'd made a mistake. So what. Hadn't we all?

I knew I could forgive her, I just needed to blank out the anger and make her realise that we could be happy together again and that going to live with Steve would be the biggest mistake she ever made. The real world and its real relationships had been shut out and her own personality had been sacrificially buried, replaced by this automaton, a genial hostess and everybody's friend, the pub landlady. There was no room in her emotions to accommodate me, or anyone else that used to matter. The lodgers had taken over, and I had had to sleep on the doorstep, waiting for scraps of attention. But it was time to change all that.

Joy smiled as we emerged from baggage reclaim.

It wasn't the smile of old, but at least it was a smile. When we'd first worked together, I had been struck by how consistently fresh and meaningful her smile was, free of cynicism, suspicion or hypocrisy. The automated mouth movement that greeted us now bore no resemblance to that genuinely happy smile, which had been absent for over a year. Bar life had certainly taken its toll.

I gave her a hug. 'Missed you,' I said, looking into her eyes. She smiled, tight-lipped.

'How you doing?' she said, ignoring the hopeful prompt and throwing her arms round Nan.

'Eee, look at you. Last time I saw you, you were *that* big,' said Nan, gesturing to knee level.

Joy smiled at me over her shoulder, raising her eyebrows. It was going to be a long three weeks.

CHAPTER THIRTEEN

To my great consternation Joy was *still* pining for Steve, waiting for the phone call that would summon her to a new life back in the UK. She'd been speaking to him on a daily basis but apparently things were 'still being sorted'. Bizarrely, I could feel her heartache, which added to the heaviness already dragging my own heart southwards.

My anger had now subsided, but the kaleidoscope of other emotions remained; in no particular order, I felt: betrayed, sad, dogged by a sense of impending doom, heartbroken, lonely, exhausted and bewildered. Oh, and full of love. As much as I tried to deny it, I knew I still loved Joy and in different circumstances we could have remained together forever.

The phone calls became less frequent over the next two weeks and Joy became increasingly despondent. Despite this, she still managed to hit the Smugglers stage running every morning, beaming with the same welcoming smile as soon as the first customer arrived for a bellyful of beans and toast. Even I got a smile most mornings as we both arrived at the bar from our respective apartments. I analysed the smile, desperate to find any clues that would lead me to believe it wasn't just her catch-all 'Smugglers' grin. Unfortunately it always was.

The mixture of emotions, combined with the not knowing whether she was actually going to leave my life forever was draining. Added to this the extra burden of making sure Nan was okay.

The days had fallen into a familiar pattern.

Morning shift then deliver meals-on-flip-flops to Nan in her top-floor Altamira apartment (prawn sandwich with crisps, small sherry on the side), quick game of dominoes, race back to our respective apartments for a shower and change of clothes just in time for evening shift. Nan would shuffle into the bar herself at about 7pm, order half a chicken and chips, two sherries and a slab of apple pie, then join David and me in the kitchen at around nine to help with the washing-up. As she was a little short, we had to lift her onto an upturned beer crate so she could reach into the deep sink. This worked fine until it came to refilling the sink, which required the use of a foot pedal Frank – our loyal DIY bodger – had installed an inconvenient 3 feet away. The combination of raised altitude and short arms meant she couldn't reach the pedal, even with the golf club the rest of us used, so every twenty minutes or so she'd yell 'Club!', her signal that we needed to come to her assistance.

The foot pedal was the legacy of just one of many new 'laws' that had been introduced in our local municipality recently. The sudden announcement that all restaurant kitchens in the region of Adeje were required to install foot-operated water taps made no sense whatsoever (especially in our case as we also needed to grasp a golf club with our mucky hands in order to reach it). We presumed that the mayor's son or other close relative had bought a boatload of plumbing gear that he wanted to shift and had asked for dad's help in ensuring he made a quick buck on it.

We'd left Frank to install the foot pedal one day

while we were out but hadn't banked on him choosing not to place it directly under the sink, where you'd expect to find your feet when washing up, but a couple of paces to the right, out of the way – and out of reach.

It was very magnanimous of Nan to volunteer in the 40-plus heat, but her presence meant that David and I had to watch our language during the final hours of the kitchen shift, which was usually the time we were both at our weariest and crankiest. Kitchen Tourette's is as much a part of the chef's life as stainless steel utensils and white floppy hats and it proved a real challenge for both of us to keep the obscenities in check.

Nan was a hard worker, despite being an octogenarian. The only time she would leave a pile of crockery unwashed was on Bingo nights. As soon as Joy started handing out the little pink sheets, Nan would dismount from her red plastic pedestal, scoop her handbag from atop the chest freezer and hurry into the busy bar to plonk herself at any table that had a spare seat. This she did with the minimum of fuss, even if the startled diners were still mid-meal. Nan wouldn't bother with introductions, she'd just sit there smiling, rummage in her bag for the Bingo dobber she always carried round and wait patiently for the numbers to be called.

We took Nan out when we could, and most of the time we brought her back too. On one occasion I left her nursing a tonic water and bag of crisps at a beachfront restaurant in Los Cristianos while I set about some extracurricular chores. David had borrowed Frank's car to tackle the tasks on his own list and he and I had arranged to meet at the bank to sign some paperwork. Our signatures were required on an unnecessarily large stack of forms, but not before each one had been explained in detail by an assistant bank manager keen to show off his grasp of English. It was one of five items on my list of things to do that day.

Lists in Tenerife and lists in the civilised world are entirely different beasts. Elsewhere they can usually be happily ticked off with an air of satisfaction. In Tenerife they're like herpes. No matter how hard you try, you just can't get rid of them.

Come the time when the sun has thrown long shadows over your challenge-filled day, with a forlorn look you flop wearily into your chair, clutching the very same list. The only alteration to it being the stains of sweat and tears from having begged, pleaded and screamed in an attempt to achieve some modicum of success on this uncooperative island.

That morning I had stared apprehensively at the list:

1. Ask for copy of statement and later sign papers at bank
2. Pick up mysterious letter from post office
3. Buy cat food for Buster
4. Get a haircut
5. Buy birthday present for Joy

I knew from hard-won experience that any task involving that four-letter word 'b-a-n-k' could throw all other plans into disarray so I decided to get the worst job out of the way first.

After dropping Nan off, finding a parking space

in Los Cristianos proved as easy as trying to find a waiter in Las Américas when you needed to pay the bill. But eventually I made it to the bank, where, as usual, my request for a duplicate bank statement was met with a look of utter incomprehension. It was as though I was the first person to ever step through their doors and ask for such a thing. The girl behind the glass screen looked everywhere – to her left, her right, under her chair – for a clue as to how to deal with this strange request, then decided that a mini interrogation was probably in order.

'Do you have some identification?'

'Yes I do.'

'Is your account at this branch?'

'It certainly was the last time I visited, but that doesn't necessarily mean it still is.' The banks had a reputation for randomly switching your account from one branch to another without thinking that it might be helpful if they informed the account holder at some point.

'Is it just your account?'

'Mine and the handful of others with whom you regularly choose to share my funds.' I still hadn't forgiven the bank for transferring funds from our account to Jack, my stepfather's account when his had insufficient money to cover a direct debit one month. 'Well you know him!' was the reasoning from the bank manager when we had confronted him.

'What did you want again?'

Eventually a torn-off piece of paper was pushed my way. It's reassuring to know that the bank is keeping its costs down in such an obvious manner – by recycling paper, employing minimal staff, offering zero training for aforementioned minimal staff and so forth.

Our appointment with the assistant bank manager wasn't for another hour so, flushed with the half-success of my first endeavour, I walked the 2 miles back to my car with a little spring of optimism in my step.

I had received indication that a document had been sent that was in urgent need of my signature and so the post office was my next port of call. After another personal pop quiz, an industrially bespectacled lady begrudgingly shuffled off in search of the letter. There followed lots of paper rustling, drawer banging and what sounded like bag-emptying before she returned empty-handed with her hair messed up and glasses slightly askew, looking as though she had fallen headlong into one of the mail sacks.

'It's not here,' she explained with a finality that suggested I was now on my own.

'Well where could it be?' I interrupted as she summoned the next in line with a curled finger.

She examined the notification letter again from over the top girder of her glasses.

'It was sent from Santa Cruz, so you could try there.'

'I'm not going up to Santa Cruz to try and find a letter that you have seemingly lost. What was it about?'

'It looks like a final electricity bill reminder or something.'

Oh great, I thought, envisaging weeks of eating by candlelight while waiting for Unelco to deem me worthy of reconnection.

'Will you ask them to send it again?' I said, by now beginning to feel a little irked.

One out of two isn't bad, I thought as I headed for the pet shop. I hated going to the pet shop – seeing all those puppies and kittens made me feel guilty for not buying them. I would find myself backing out, silently apologising to each and every cage. But there was no alternative: I was after a hundredweight of high-protein, low-calorie, easily digestible biscuits for Buster. We'd had to put him on a diet as his daily intake of raw meat had given him the physique of a furry beach ball and we feared there was a real possibility he could burst.

That particular food wasn't in stock so I toyed with the idea of taking him something different, but I knew he'd only turn his back, refuse to talk to me for several days and revert to chewing on the legs of our customers. So it was back to the beef and chicken for a few more days.

One out of three still wasn't too bad, but then it turned into one out of four and the day started to drag my spirits down into that all too familiar murky pit of despair. Apparently everybody and their dog, cat and pet monkey wanted a haircut over the next four weeks and I wasn't about to trust a total stranger with the task of creating my delicately styled 'just-got-out-of-the-washing-machine-look' that my regular hairdresser was so adept at.

Buying a present for Joy was not going to be easy, I already knew that. Although overloaded with hotels and British bars, south Tenerife is a monoculture when it comes to shops. All the guidebooks describe the Canary Islands as a region of the utmost diversity. If you're looking for a range of landscapes, then yes, this is true. If, however, you want a selection of different outlets from which to choose birthday presents, it is not.

Items of clothing broadcasting the location of purchase were never Joy's first choice in fashion, which ruled out all the Tenerife T-shirts and sweatshirts. Beach towels imprinted with profiles of Elvis or Spanish football icons also didn't make the list, and nor did sombreros, fake watches, boxed orchids or bottles of banana liquor. Which didn't leave an awful lot of options.

Many times I'd departed from Los Cristianos or Las Américas empty-handed and with frustrated resignation after realising on the eve of yet another birthday that the only present I was going to offer would be made from recycled paper and wrapped in a plain white envelope. It looked like that was going to happen again, but at least I hadn't left it to the last minute this time.

To be fair, the shopping situation had improved a little over the last couple of years. If it was Stinging Nettle Genital Scrub or Loganberry Corn Plasters that your loved one couldn't do without, then at least we now had our own Body Shop. Mere days after the opening of this particular shop in Los Cristianos my bathroom in El Beril became inundated with these weird and wonderful cocktails that provided dubious bodily benefit for Joy. My personal vanity area had been pushed to a far corner behind the vegetarian ear products and anti-wrinkle syrups, a lone toothbrush in a plastic cup valiantly flying the flag for male toiletries.

Back then, if I got the munchies in the middle of the night I didn't know whether to reach for the kitchen cupboard or the bathroom shelf. I often wondered, if they can turn edibles into enhancers, why will it not work the other way round? Why are we not able to season salads with soothing skin lotions and spread after-sun butter on Jacob's crackers? Progress is inevitable so surely the next step is to combine those household chores that inhibit our quest for career advancement with other domestic rituals. How about food steamers that you can place in the suds while you're reclining in the bath? Add a little sesame oil and a handful of basil to the water and a tasty dinner awaits the moment you pull the plug. Economical and time-saving! Surely a hit with anyone struggling to meet deadlines yet keen to maintain a healthy diet.

Show me a shop with that kind of innovative product in Tenerife and you'd have my trade for the next decade at least. Joy, however, was not going to be so lucky. And anyway, it was time to revisit the bank for my rendezvous with David.

The signing of papers and subsequent explanation of every clause, sub-clause and sub-sub-clause went as well as could be expected but left us very little time to get back and prepare the Smugglers for opening. Outside the bank we headed to our separate car parks and sped back to El Beril. It was ten past one by the time we got there and already there were two families sitting waiting outside. Joy was already inside, restocking the beer fridge. When she saw we'd returned, she flicked the lights and music on, laid out the ashtrays and beer mats and told the waiting customers that we'd be with them in a minute. David changed a beer barrel and loaded the ice bucket behind the bar. In the kitchen I fired up the four rings and central hotplate, plugged in the chip fryer and hoped that we wouldn't have too much of a rush after the initial early-birds. Thankfully we didn't and at quarter past three, having served the two families with drinks and meals, we had time to sit at the bar and discuss possible ways to bring in more money.

'What about advertising on the radio?' I offered.

'Nah... Too much money and we're too far away from civilisation,' said David. 'What about putting the prices up?'

'Maybe,' I pondered. 'We might get away with it.'

Joy looked at the clock. 'Nan's late.'

'She'll be here in a bit,' I said. 'What about a barbecue night? Mario used to do them when he owned the bar and apparently they were a bit hit.'

'Hmm, not a bad idea,' said David.

'What about Nan?' said Joy.

'How can she help?' said David.

'We could send her out with flyers,' I joked.

'Or get her to stroll round in a sandwich board,' said David.

'No, you numpts! Was she alright when you dropped her off, David?'

He shook his head. 'I didn't drop her off. Joe did.' They both turned to look at me.

I jumped off the stool. 'Shit. I thought *you* were getting her.'

'She's still down there!' shrieked Joy.

'Shit, shit, shit!' I shouted. I threw my apron into the kitchen and grabbed the car keys from the hook under the first-aid box.

I reached Los Cristianos in less than ten minutes, screeched to a halt in the harbour car park and ran along the promenade to where we'd left Nan. She was still sitting in the same spot, calmly watching the world go by, nursing the same tonic water we'd left her with four hours ago.

'Hello,' she chirped. 'Thought you'd forgotten about me for a minute.' She winked. 'Are you ready to go?'

~

Nan had made a few friends in the Altamira who had taken to calling in for a game of dominoes. She had decided that there was more fun to be had when money was involved and unbeknown to us had started charging 100 pesetas to join a game, with winner-take-all pots.

We only found out when Joy and I called in one day to deliver a slice of freshly baked apple pie. We could hear shouting from beyond the door.

'You daft beggar, that's not a seven it's an eight.' It was Nan's voice. 'Take it back or I'll thump you.'

Joy and I looked at each other in puzzlement.

Inside, five pensioners were sitting around the glass-topped coffee table, each with stacks of coins in front of them.

'Aha!' smiled Joy. 'Busted!'

Nan had been in Tenerife for three weeks by then. She'd already told us that she had enjoyed her stay but, despite her new friends and the dominoes, she was ready to go home. Joy had immediately volunteered to escort her back to the UK but we'd decided David should go instead. I suspected Joy had ulterior motives and knew that she'd undoubtedly go and see Steve – and possibly would not return.

Once the gambling pensioners had left for the afternoon, Joy and I started to tidy up Nan's apartment. 'David's booked you a ticket back to England, Nan,' I shouted as Joy and I folded bloomers and bras that she'd hung over the balcony. 'He's going to take you back.'

Nan waddled out to join us. 'Good,' she said, mopping her brow with a lacy handkerchief. 'Need to have me boobs checked anyway.'

'Oh, right. What do you mean?'

'Been having a problem with this one.' Nan plunged an arm down the front of her sundress, pulled out a prosthesis and tossed it towards Joy. Joy, startled by both the announcement and at having a false boob thrown her way, failed to catch the airborne jelly. The silicone implant disappeared over the railings and fell six storeys onto the grass below.

'Beggar!' said Nan.

We watched over the railings as a young boy in swimming trunks pick up the prosthesis, turned it over in his hands, then skipped off towards the pool, throwing it up and down.

'I'm definitely going to have to go and get it checked, now,' said Nan calmly.

CHAPTER FOURTEEN

February is Carnival season in Tenerife, a time when half the island participates in the giant parades, all-day and all-night drinking and incessant partying, and the other half complains about the noise and lack of productivity. February 1995 saw Joy and me in no frame of mind to party. Joy's mood was sullen. She had long given up on Steve making good on his promise to summon her back for a life in the UK – God knows how many other girls he'd been with since he'd left our sub-tropical shores. My spirits were clouded too: even though she had stopped waiting for Steve, there still didn't feel like a whole lot of hope for a reunion between Joy and me.

One shiny ray of light was that Wayne was back with us again, our pot-smoking, gas engineer who in our early days at the Smugglers had come to our rescue after Frank's potentially disastrous tinkering with the gas tank. Wayne wanted nothing more out of life than a smooth path and a laugh with his mates. He had no aspirations, no self-delusion and called a spade whatever he damn well wanted to call it.

Since the last time he'd been over, he'd dumped his girlfriend and had decided to meander between Wolverhampton and El Beril as the mood took him. Pushy yet sociable, he always found some sort of work, be it fixing expats' cars, mending household appliances or even taming explosive gas canisters.

In his infinite wisdom, and as is the way with

boys, Wayne had decided that all I needed to get out of the doldrums was a good night out. Carnival was the obvious opportunity, but his plans involved one element that worried me. He'd also decided that a night out was what Joy needed too and so he'd arranged for Joy and Sammy to meet us when we got there. The prospect of seeing Joy dancing or being hit on by someone else was not overly appealing but I realised it was something I was going to have to get used to.

Wayne had made no effort to hide his sadness when Joy and I split up and although we'd now been apart for almost ten months he'd not given up in his campaign to get us back together. I, however, considered it a very remote possibility. Naturally, Joy was upset that her plans for an easy life with Steve in his English mansion had fallen through, but there had been no signs that she wanted to try and continue where we'd left off, even though she had been decidedly more friendly with me recently, and I with her.

There was another major drawback to Wayne's plan. It involved fancy dress, which was pretty much compulsory for anybody attending Carnival. I have never seen the appeal of dressing up as something you're not, then trying to remain in that role for hours at a time. Yes, I know you call this theatre, but being a contented introvert, my place in the theatre is reclining on a faux-velvet seat with a bucket of popcorn while a host of other giddy kippers cavort in the limelight. So, to cushion the embarrassment of the fancy dress, we were going to start the evening off by first heading downtown for 'a livener', as Wayne put it.

Wayne's response to my depression was typically male – he offered the bottle. Women faced with girlfriends in a similar situation, I've noticed, often head straight to the kettle instead. Neither remedy is truly medicinal of course, but given the choice, I'd opt for Kentucky bourbon over PG Tips every time.

What took me by surprise was just how unprepared I was – in all ways – for a big night out. Even though my wardrobe space had doubled in size since Joy had moved out, in the words of Mother Hubbard, 'the cupboard was bare'. Well, not exactly bare. It *was* furnished with a ginger mop that had curled cosily around my black loafers and now blinked up at me half asleep.

Since Joy had left, Buster had sensed my loneliness and regularly followed me back home at the end of a shift, disappearing somewhere inside the apartment for hours on end and then suddenly reappearing magically like the Cheshire Cat. Earlier in the week he'd gone missing for two days. It was only when I opened a cupboard door to throw a beer can in the rubbish bin at 3am that I discovered him sitting upright under the sink, calmly waiting for an opportunity to be released.

Apart from the cat, a pitiful pile of sun-faded shorts and T-shirts that had seen too many seasons occupied the remaining wardrobe space, with a pair of white jeans and a sleeveless buttoned vest the only concession to the world of haute couture.

It felt odd not having anyone there to offer advice in the fashion department. I'd always needed it. Being colour blind means that my ability to sport complementary tones is limited. On numerous occasions in the past I'd only been saved from going out dressed in clothes that could have led to merciless teasing and quite possibly a public stoning by an eleventh-hour intervention from Joy, so you can imagine the anguish I was going through. However, white and cream was safe, I thought, as I tried to convince myself that I looked okay in the mirror.

I was ready an hour and a half before we were due to go out. The couple of steadying Jack Daniels I'd downed while cagily trying out a few dance moves had raised a hunger issue so I decided to phone for a sneaky pizza from our regular 'supplier'.

'Hello, I'd like to order a pizza please.'

'Sorry?'

'A pizza. I'd like to order one, to be delivered please.'

'A pizza? I don't understand. Can you phone back?'

Five seconds later, 'Hello, I'd like to order a pizza please,' I repeated, a little more forcefully this time.

'Okay. Who is it for?'

'It's for Joe in El Beril. You've delivered here many times before.'

'Nope. Don't know you. Beryl, you say?'

'No, I'm Joe. El Beril is where I live.'

We agreed that my name wasn't Beryl and I gave my contact details and account number to him again.

'I'd like a large Fiery Meat Pizza with no olives but extra pineapple and a few capers.'

'Okay.' The phone slammed down.

An hour later I put down the soggy cushion I'd been chewing and phoned back.

'Hello. I ordered a pizza an hour ago and it's still not arrived.' I gave him my details again but any previous knowledge of my existence had been deleted from his dough-frazzled memory.

'Sorry. The man who usually makes the pizza bases is out at the moment,' replied the voice.

'Out? Well when's he back?'

'Two weeks. He's gone on holiday. Poland, I think. Or was it Portugal?'

'That's all very interesting, but is there any chance I can have a pizza?'

'Sure. Twenty minutes. I can make it.'

I repeated my order again and put the phone down, shaking my head.

Thirty minutes later there was a knock on my door. A large helmet with a pair of spindly legs sticking out pushed a flat box towards me.

'Nine hundred pesetas,' demanded the helmet with gloved hand outstretched.

I paid, and eagerly anticipating the hot aroma of melted cheese, lifted the cardboard lid to discover a cold pizza that looked like the topping had been fired from a distant cannon. Even amid the carnage I could see that it quite clearly wasn't anything like the pizza I'd ordered.

Deeply disappointed and now ravenous enough to eat the cardboard box, I phoned back to complain.

'Where's my capers?' I barked.

'Erm... the capers come from Gran Canaria and we have to order them specially. I can send them on when they arrive if you like?'

'And when would that be?'

'April. Maybe end of March if you're lucky,' the man answered calmly.

'This isn't the pizza I ordered,' I continued.

'The delivery boy is blind. He can't see which pizzas he's delivering.'

'But he rides a moped!'

'I know. It's a wonder you got *any* pizza. I'd think yourself lucky, mate.' The phone went dead again.

Resignedly, I turned round to find Buster standing ankle deep in the pizza, licking tomato puree from his furry cheeks. At least somebody had enjoyed it.

At that moment the doorbell rang and Wayne strode in, dressed in white shirt, black jeans, cowboy boots and bootlace tie.

'Are we going to a hoe-down?' I said.

'Cheeky fucker,' he smiled, offering a swig of the cheap whisky bottle he was carrying. 'You up for it?'

'Bring it on,' I lied.

~

During the 10-minute taxi ride to Las Americas, Wayne and I discussed the various merits of individual beers. Fosters was his tipple of choice. I was more loyal to the local brew, Dorada. 'Why don't we do a beer test, then?' suggested Wayne. 'Try a different one in each bar.' It made perfect sense to me. We decided that there were enough beak-nosed whisky-sniffers and snooty wine-spitters around. It was time to give beer the same experimental treatment. But, as is the case when two males come up with a plan that involves alcohol, we spent the last remaining minutes in the taxi complicating things with a series of rules.

1. We were only to have one half beer or one bottle in each bar.

2. In between beers we had to eat something bland to clear the way for the next beer.

3. At least one of us had to remember to get the bus up to Santa Cruz to meet Sammy and Joy.

After paying the taxi fare, we headed into one of the rip-off supermarkets embedded in the Veronicas nightlife strip and paid a small fortune for a block of Cheshire cheese. Why cheese? I have no idea, but it was the first thing that either of us could think of that was remotely bland, so Wayne stuffed it into his rucksack along with our fancy dress attire and we set off on our fact-finding mission.

At Bosbies Nightclub the beat banged incessantly inside my skull; the kind of repetitive trance-inducing rhythm that seems to bother you less if you nod up and down, zombie-like. Any communication took a great deal of lip-reading and mimicry, which, to give them credit, the bar staff had become very adept at deciphering.

The lighting, or more accurately 'darking' varied between pitch black and a flickering fluorescence, capturing the dancers in jerky, black and white freeze-frames. A group of girls dressed in flimsy white arrived and immediately began to dance uninhibitedly, until one of them presumably noticed that the X-ray effect of the lighting was making their underwear glow like radioactive twinsets. I smiled as they hurried out. When the light permitted, it was entertaining to watch the facial expressions, not to mention the knicker revelations – until I remembered that I too had chosen white. Sure enough, my two-year-old boxers shone the light for Marks and Spencer's, clear for all to see.

In the world of club wear, less is definitely more. Two girls gyrating nearby wore nothing more than hot pants and push-up bras, a far call from the shy shuffling of my school disco days, when provocative dressing involved girls leaving their cardigans unbuttoned. There were, however, some sights that even the most creative imagination couldn't transfigure – the girls with the distorted mirrors. These size 20s had seemingly looked at their reflections and thought that by trussing themselves up tightly with bits of string and Lycra, they could fool themselves and others into thinking that a 20-pound turkey could disguise itself as a 4-ounce quail.

The only people who had decent vision in this black world were the water-bearing, teeth-grinding night-trippers whose pupils had expanded to the size of small coins. They knew that any ticket to ride was available in this darkness. Whatever your poison, just ask and ye shall receive. In fact if you were to corner a PR and discreetly murmur an insatiable desire for 2 pounds of pork sausages, a friend of a friend would know someone and within minutes, over a disguised handshake, offal would be shoved up your sleeve, money exchanged and the fixer would slink back into the dark, eager to search out the next customer.

Back on the dance floor, a group of young lads

were being watched carefully by the bouncers as they jigged awkwardly around a pretty girl dancing alone. Long strands of black hair curtained her face as hips swayed provocatively, eyes fixed firmly on her bare feet. She seemed lost in the music, unaware of the group of admirers closing in with their stilted movements.

Why is it that with the exception of Latinos and Afro-Caribbeans, men just cannot dance? Women can get every extremity of their bodies to perform with rhythmic sensuality, but men twitch and jerk as if each limb is possessed by a different demon while hopping from side to side dodging an imaginary stampede.

Wayne and I finished the first beers (Heineken), rated them as top class, and took a bite of cheese ready for the next tasting. We were just about to leave when our exit was blocked by a torrent of youngsters pouring through the door in a never-ending conga; they were on one of Tenerife's many organised 'pub crawls'. Being seen downtown in one of these school chain set-ups must be almost embarrassing as being spotted riding the numpty train through Las Américas. Why would anybody want to be told where to go, what to drink and how long you have to drink it, and then pay over the odds for the privilege?

Over the next hour or so we moved from one bar to the next sampling San Miguel, Dorada, Carlsberg, Budweiser, Tropical, Fosters and Coors. By this stage logic and sense had jumped ship leaving both our brains drifting in a sea of alcohol like boats without a captain.

Consequently it was decided that pints would

allow us more of a chance to savour the delights of each beer. This in turn led to an attack of the munchies and the remainder of the cheese was messily devoured. Things then took a distinct turn for the worst as void of any palate cleansers we, quite reasonably at the time, determined that vodka shots would provide the same cleansing qualities and we flopped ourselves down at yet another bar.

'Two pintsh of a beer that we haven't already tried yet,' I directed roughly in the direction of two identical barmen who both seemed eager to serve us. The twins produced what appeared to be four pints and set them in front of us. 'What ish it?' I asked turning to my fellow researcher.

After a slight pause, just long enough for the room to do a couple of circuits around us, Wayne answered helpfully, 'beer.' I nodded sagely and we both agreed that it was good.

'Two vots of shodka,' I ordered to nobody in particular, adding, 'have you shot any geese?' This appeared to have amused Wayne to the extent that he was now giggling from the floor having toppled off his stool. I tried again. 'I mean...have...you...got...enemy...sheese?' I was at that stage where my lips would not meet and my head would not be still and decided that enough was enough. A man could only contribute so much to the world of science and research in one night. Plus, remarkably but a little vaguely, I was still aware that we had rendezvous plans in the north. But first, more food was needed.

Under the watchful gaze of the security man we staggered into Macdonalds for a well-earned snack. 'Two double long whopper cheesy things with no green stuff, extra bacon or barbecue sauce,' I said to the young girl, eyes black and bleary with having to deal with drunks such as us night after night. She leaned forward a little, contempt clearly evident in her frown and tight lips and asked if I could repeat my order. Clearly I couldn't so I just looked at her pathetically.

'What do you want?' she asked with a sigh.

'That,' I said feebly, pointing a finger at the menu board behind her.

'With cheese?' I nodded inanely.

'Anything else... sir?' I noted the long pause before the word 'sir', shook my head and offered her a handful of screwed up money. Wayne and I turned to leave then spent several moments wondering why we had been locked in as we struggled with the glass door, him pushing, me pulling.

In front of the Veronicas strip, the scene was apocalyptic. The place was littered with beer bottles, plastic cups and kebab wrappers. Bodies were strewn everywhere, some crying, some staring glassy-eyed into oblivion, one or two lying unconscious next to lumpy pools of their own vomit. This was a normal end-of-night in Veronicas. The drinks over-priced, the drinkers under-age, the drugs over the counter, the music overbearing and the bins overflowing. To all intents and purposes, it's a downright disgusting mess, but despite the chaotic aftermath, Veronicas, and many other similar destinations throughout the world, still draw teenage holidaymakers in their thousands.

For Wayne and me, it wasn't the end of the night, however; it was merely the warm-up to what lay a forty minute bus ride up the motorway to Santa Cruz.

~

For such a macho culture, Tenerife is surprisingly well endowed with men happy to dress up in the cheerier attire of the softer sex. With so much testosterone-fuelled competitiveness, perhaps Carnival serves as a necessary release from the customary chauvinism and laddish behaviour.

Amazingly, the bus ride had a sobering effect and after having changed into fancy dress behind the bus station, Wayne and I added daubs of make-up to each other, then followed the throngs to the heart of the action. As arranged, we headed to a bar to meet up with Joy and Sammy, who were both dressed as mob gangsters. I have to admit that on this occasion I did enjoy the opportunity to wear something that had a little more colour and was just a touch more revealing than my normal outfits. Cherry red was not a shade that I wore often, especially in the form of a top-of-the-thighs mini-dress. Still, it matched my lipstick and provided a nice contrast to the black fishnet stockings, which, I have to say, were worryingly comfortable.

To cross-dress *and* dance to an alien beat would naturally require a great deal more alcoholic assistance and it was with this in mind that we inched towards one of the outdoor bars on the edge of the Plaza de España. On a normal day, it was easy to stroll from one plaza café to another, mooching at the handcrafted linens, Teide snow shakers and other Tenerife souvenirs in shop windows along the way. But now there were thousands of people rubbing elbows, all with one common aim in mind: to enjoy *la vida loca* – the crazy life – until the small hours.

Carnival in Tenerife is massive, the island's biggest social event by far. For fifteen days every February the city of Santa Cruz grinds to a near halt as Carnival queens are paraded and satirical pantomimes performed; big bands boom out raucous beats and city workers shut up shop to save their energy for sundown when the party proper starts.

Some claim that Tenerife's Carnival is second only to Rio's. In fact, in 1987, the Santa Cruz Carnival was mentioned in the *Guinness Book of Records* for hosting the largest open-air dance, with over 200,000 people collectively shaking their funky stuff at one time. It's become something of an island obsession to participate in these festivities, which date back to the Spanish Conquest in the late fifteenth century. Nearly every year since then, the celebrations have proceeded in one form or another. Even during the turbulent times of Franco, when 'Carnival' was banned, Tenerife simply renamed it 'the Winter Festival' and carried on regardless.

One of the biggest events is the crowning of the Carnival Queen, the climax of incessant TV interviews and costume-strutting. A great deal of blood, sweat and creativity – plus the occasional hissy fit – goes into the design of the colossal dresses, with the contest just as much about the garment as it is about the girl.

During the afternoons, extravagant floats

accompanied by musicians and dancers parade under the eclectic mix of new and old architecture along the shorefront Avenida Maritima. Costumes push the boundaries of elegance and enormity, with head-dresses reaching higher than the palm trees lining the avenue.

While daytimes are more about watching, when night falls so do the inhibitions. Pockets of tourists that have travelled from all over the globe are conspicuous among the throngs of lithe, hip-swaying locals. Struggling to synchronise their limbs with the unfamiliar Latin beat, they find themselves stuck between repeating the mechanical movements of a school barn dance and bobbing up and down like someone at the wrong end of a lengthy toilet queue, dancing a dance that is definitely more ketchup than salsa.

Cacophonous beats burst from live bands in every plaza. Kiosks festooned with coloured bulbs keep the throngs supplied with copious amounts of alcohol, sizzling cuts of meat and sweet pastries. The barrage of noise and kaleidoscope of colour is hypnotic and it's impossible not to be drawn into the party spirit. The only ones who stand out are those who aren't in some kind of fancy dress, but at Carnival they're always few and far between.

They say a good party will bring out the best in anybody, but participating in Tenerife's biggest celebration didn't exactly reflect my own mood. I can't deny the frivolity didn't help a little, but it was the first party I'd been to without Joy for over a decade and there was no hiding behind her bubbly personality this time. Joy was Joy, and I was Joe. And now I had to stand on my own two feet socially – even if those two feet were already complaining about exceptionally narrow shoes and teetering heels.

Taped music from over a hundred outdoor bars competed against the many bands dotted around the Plaza de España and the adjoining Plaza de la Candelaria, producing a head-spinning riot of salsa rhythms. Wayne and Sammy duly disappeared into the crowd, fuelled with Bacardi, weed and poppers, and I headed for the nearest drinks stall. A nun with a thick black moustache sucked in his stomach and lifted his arms to allow me to pass. From one hand, Marlboro ash drifted down like confetti, and from the other, the contents of a plastic glass rained onto the hood of his devotional partner, bringing forth a burst of slurred Spanish that I suspected contained quite a few sacred references.

The crowd around the brightly lit refreshment kiosk was four deep and from behind a pungent leg of cured ham I tried in vain to get the attention of the sunken-eyed barmen, their white shirts completely drenched from having served endless plastic tumblers of *cubatas* (rum and Coke) and plates of *churros* (deep-fried doughnuts) in the heavy heat of the Canarian night.

I had left Joy near the row of delightfully named *pipís moviles* (mobile toilets), and returned with drinks in hand just in time to see her being whisked into the mêlée by an old man bearing an uncanny resemblance to the late Walter Matthau. She waved a not altogether happy greeting as her surprisingly athletic companion tossed her from side to side. I raised a glass to toast her new-found friendship and the toast was returned with the mouthing of a word pertaining to having no father.

It was also returned by the most exquisite female form that I have ever had the boldness to raise a glass to, on purpose or inadvertently. She was some three feet beyond Joy and Walter, her tall slender body provocatively curved and arched under the spell of Latin fever. I realised that I might have been standing with my mouth ajar for several minutes and snapped it shut, swallowing hard as the girl shimmered towards me.

'*Quieres bailar?*'

As Joy was obviously preoccupied, and my current decision-making ability was powered by more than a little rum, I nodded that I would indeed like to dance and set the two glasses at the foot of a short but expansive silver laurel whose glossy green canopy had been gaily festooned with crisscrossed strings of coloured lightbulbs.

There followed many hazy minutes spent inhaling pheromone-flooded perfume and shuffling face to face with a perfect blend of doe-eyed innocence and deep-tanned allure, all the while performing intimate gyrations that, but for the absence of a fleecy bedsheet and the presence of a hundred thousand onlookers, could have plausibly been called sex. Only after quite some time did I realise that Joy must by now be tiring of the windscreen-wiper choreography of Mr Matthau and was probably in danger of suffering whiplash.

I motioned apologetically that I had to leave and went to rescue Joy, but not before the girl clasped the back of my head, pressed soft lips onto mine and thrust a probing tongue deep into my lungs. Startled, to say the least, I backed away, grabbing

146

her hands and lowering them to a safer level. It was at this point that the words 'What the…?' were hastily passed from brain to mouth.

An unmistakable carpet of hair furnished the back of her, or as I now alarmingly realised, *his* hands. The salsa became slurred; a hundred thousand people turned to stare and visions of hairy legs of cured ham flooded my mind. I quickly sidled off into the masses, grabbed Joy by the wrist and shouldered my way through the crowd to the nearest provider of steadying *cubatas*.

I didn't mention anything to Joy as I was too busy getting my head round what had possibly looked to bystanders like a lesbian seduction scene. The stuff of fantasy usually, but not when it involved me being one of the lesbians and the object of my affections being neither lesbian nor even female.

I spent the next half hour trying to look as menacing as one could when wearing fishnet stockings and cherry-red lipstick.

As the *cubatas* flowed, so did the conversation between Joy and me.

'It's easy to forget about the bar when you're in the middle of all this,' said Joy, gazing at the 3am melee, still going at full throttle. The plaza, side streets and bars were getting busier by the hour as young Tenerifians joined in the public frenzy, fired up from swigging booze from the boots of cars at private *botellon* parties. 'How good would it be not to have to go back to working in the bar tomorrow.'

'Do you think we'd have split up if we didn't have the bar?' I said.

Joy stared into her plastic glass of rum and Coke.

'I don't know,' she said after a few moments. 'Nobody knows. Maybe we met too soon, maybe I just needed to feel like *me* for a while.' She looked away along the low wall we were sitting on.

'And *do* you?'

'Do I what?'

'Feel like *you* now?'

Joy pondered again. 'I think I *do*,' she nodded.

I pulled off one of my high heels and rubbed my foot. 'How can you *wear* these!' I decided to take a gamble. 'Where does that leave you and Steve?'

'He's just a mummy's boy,' said Joy, smiling. 'It was a huge, huge mistake.'

'Can't say I didn't warn you!' I nudged her playfully. 'And us? Where does it leave us?'

'I don't know.' Joy looked me straight in the eye. 'Do you think it can work?'

I gave the slightest of shrugs. 'We can try.'

'I want to – if you'll have me back?'

'Let's give it a go, then,' I said.

'Come here, you big numpt,' said Joy, and she sidled over. I swear Carnival fireworks exploded the moment we hugged. Or maybe that was just my imagination.

~

We returned to El Beril just as the sun was yawning above the mountain tops. I had an hour to shower and change out of my frock while Joy went to her apartment to get ready.

We'd agreed to carry on living separately for a while so we could take things slowly and build up again from scratch. It felt like the start of a whole

148

new relationship, not the reparation of something broken. There was nothing unusual about that morning's activities but there was a noticeable lightness in many respects: gravity had eased off, making every step and movement less effort; the kitchen was more brightly illuminated, as though somebody had swapped the 30-watt, grease-smothered fluorescent tube with a brand-new 100-watt bulb; and instead of the eye-stinging, dizzy feeling that usually followed sleepless nights, my mind was fresh, alert and receptive to every little sensory stimulant. Bottles of beer clinked against each other like Christmas bells in the metallic interior as Joy restocked the bar fridge. The sweetness of freshly peeled apples fused with the warm waft of chickens roasting in the oven, producing a comforting aroma that I'd lived with every day for almost four years but only now could appreciate.

Life was back on track. Several days later Joy moved back into Number 85 and Steve and her affair faded into a dim memory. We had a long way to go to heal any wounds and rebuild trust but we were at least on the road to recovery, together again.

I knew that our relationship would never get back to the way it was before, but that was not necessarily a bad thing. We'd both changed, broken the chains that had bound us into one. It was growth, and bizarrely a strengthening experience in that I'd tasted life without Joy, and survived. I now knew I wasn't totally reliant on her, nor she on me.

Like two separate entities that had been melded together for years, we'd been pulled apart and forced to examine ourselves, and had now become two distinct personalities once more. We were very much in love again, but it was a more mature love. We knew now how important it was to be aware of each other's needs.

We had also come to realise that it was near impossible for any couple to work together under such intense pressure for that long and maintain a give-and-take relationship. Although we were happy right now, we both knew that once the novelty of getting back together had faded we could easily slip back into resenting the situation we were trapped in. Things needed to change, and drastically.

We talked about one of us getting a job elsewhere, but we both knew that the only real solution was to get out of these relationship-killing conditions completely. However, with a huge debt still hanging around our necks and our contractual binding to David, this was still impossible. Although Joy and I had emerged from the break-up personally stronger, the endurance challenge we had taken on was by no means finished yet. The actual *business* was next in line to be tested.

PART TWO

JOE CAWLEY

Chapter Fifteen

After muddling our way through broken relationships, inept catering skills and a business strategy based on the 'make it up as we go along' model, it wasn't until around June 1996, five years into our careers, that we truly felt we'd mastered the finer points of running a bar/restaurant. We began to share our nuggets of experience with other expat landlords and landladies that sat at the Smugglers bar.

'Use a fork to unblock vomit-congested urinals,' we'd suggest. 'Much better than a finger.'

'Tell Coca-Cola you're switching to Pepsi. Always good for a few free mixers and a nice new set of parasols.'

'On no account charge the police for any drinks, even if they're off-duty.'

We still had no solution to getting the last customers to drink up and leave before daybreak. Tactics such as mopping their feet, switching all the lights off and standing over them with menacing glares and folded arms made little difference. We also tried more traditional methods, which included enthusiastically ringing a large 'last orders' brass bell that a sympathetic landlord from Gillingham had brought us recently. None worked quite as well as simply snatching the drinks from under them and actually pushing them out the door with physical force, a strategy regularly demonstrated by the staff at the Altamira bar across the road. But being British, such blunt gestures were way beyond us.

While we had been silently congratulating

ourselves on finally having got to grips with this pub malarkey, the world, as it often does, conspired to change the playing field again. The bar was still the same, still home from home for its bored and boozed-up regulars. Frank was still viewing the world through slate-tinted spectacles and wishing that all the foreigners would go home. Friedhelm still occupied the up-ended beer barrel near the door, wheezing on Kruger cigarettes, staring forlornly into foamy pints and croaking to anybody who would listen about his assorted 'big problem' medical conditions. New waves of wide-eyed holidaymakers washed into the bar on a weekly basis, demanding a little bit of Britain in the sun – English telly, British beer and 'none of that foreign muck'. And our menagerie of indoor wildlife numbering Buster, an unobtrusive family of mice and a very obtrusive population of cockroaches still kept us active with a water pistol, mousetraps and domestic napalm respectively.

But while our bubble of insanity remained intact, the outside world changed once more – almost overnight.

The first evidence of this was when the holiday company Airtours pulled out of the Altamira just before the summer of 96. Apparently a dispute with the owners of the aparthotel over the number of rooms being allocated to the timeshare company resulted in them taking their ball and going somewhere else to play. Along with their ball, Airtours also took our main source of income. We had been feeding in the region of two- to three hundred of the tour operator's customers a week during the busy periods. And then, all of a sudden, we weren't.

The Smugglers Tavern was by now well known in the south, having been established for some time, two years under the guidance of Mario and now five years with David, Joy and me at the helm. It was pleasing that the bar was mentioned in the Airtours brochure as one of the 'excellent facilities' on hand for holidaymakers choosing the Altamira. Partly because of this endorsement and printed pre-sell, the vast majority of their guests happily opted to empty their pockets in our bar rather than Tel's, the Arancha or the Altamira hotel bar. But now, with our till no longer ringing to the tune of Airtours holidaymakers, it was in imminent danger of slipping into melancholic melodies forever, and with the best part of £100,000 still to pay back, that would not be a good thing at all.

Could what was once considered one of our prize assets – our isolated location – actually have become our downfall? When the Altamira and El Beril were full, so were we. But when they were empty, we didn't have enough patrons travelling from other parts of the south to sustain payments on the immense debt we'd taken on.

Truth be told, apart from a healthy dose of cussing, there wasn't a great lot that we could do about the deficiency of holidaymakers. The only other regular intake of potential patrons was the hordes of excited but naive couples flown in on a weekly basis, unwitting fodder for the fly-buy timeshare machine.

On the promise of 'free accommodation in Tenerife' (they had to pay for their own flights), the troop of pale-faced holidaymakers that were drill-marched off the coach every Friday evening agreed to attend a 'presentation', an event that in the glossy brochure was preceded by adjectives such as 'brief', 'friendly', 'fun' and 'no-pressure'. But of course it was actually the opposite – unless you call four hours of being lectured to as 'brief'; understand 'friendly' to be having complete strangers interrogate you about your personal wealth; and consider heavy-handed, arm-twisting coercion as 'no-pressure'.

Joy and I had first-hand experience of this pleasure. In fact, several experiences. Long before the idea of committing full-time to the island was raised we had decided to while away some winter weeks in my Mum's apartment on El Beril. While there, we cottoned on to an 'easy' means of adding to our measly amount of spending money; we had just £200, which we'd hoped would last six weeks but in reality lasted around three. As we were therefore more or less surviving on handouts from departing holidaymakers we'd befriended at the Altamira, our own personal timeshare plan looked like it would enable us to stay in Tenerife an extra week or two.

The timeshare set-up works pretty much like the food chain. Bottom-feeders (street PRs) hook in unsuspecting holidaymakers with scratch cards promising untold riches – or, more important to the British, free booze. The 'winners' are then shoved into a taxi and spat out at a timeshare resort, where the prize has to be collected from the next level of predators.

The sales sharks circle holidaymakers during their tour of the timeshare resort, all the while befriending you, asking about your job, hobbies, family and the place you live. Then they use this info in a tailor-made sales pitch which is rained down on you as you wait at a table for your freebies; meanwhile, champagne corks are popped sporadically at other tables, 'implying' that sales have just been made and you're missing out on something.

After ninety minutes of being worn down, your every objection countered, you might eventually say you simply can't afford it. Then the bigger sharks are let loose. The timeshare managers are brought in, offering an even lower price and the objection/counter-objection cycle begins again as they snap at you with cutting comments and coercive questions like 'We're trying to save you some money here. Don't you want to save money on your holidays?'

If you somehow survive that round of mauling, the great whites are let loose, the closers. They also have a bite at extracting money, only releasing you with a four-quid bottle of cheap spirits when you sign a form acknowledging receipt of your prize and committing to a mailbox deluge of further printed pressure.

Admittedly things have changed for the better over the years. The sharks are now made to keep their distance, and although still intimidating, they've been muzzled to a certain extent, banned from using certain unscrupulous sales techniques.

While on our extended holiday all those years ago, we had got talking to Mark, one of the bottom-feeders, during a stroll along the front in Playa de las Américas. Joy being Joy had found out all about his personal life history and current job situation. Bottom-feeders were paid £50 for every married couple they could deliver off the street to the timeshare resorts. The best could get five couples a morning, using ploys such as telling the husband and wife they were trying to get back to their sick mother in the UK and needed just one more 'sale' to afford the plane ticket home. Or saying that they were really bad at this job and if they didn't get one more couple up to the resort they were going to be fired and made homeless.

Joy suggested to Mark that he could send us on one of these timeshare presentations and split the commission. He'd get his £25 and we'd get our £25 plus a free bottle of spirits. How hard could it be?

'Here, stick this on,' Mark said to Joy, handing her his own ring. 'They only accept married couples.'

He gave us a ticket to claim our prize and inform the company that we were his clients and Joy and I then travelled five minutes to the timeshare resort in a pre-paid taxi. The tour and presentation passed in a whirl of non-committal nods, ending with Joy announcing, 'We're never going to buy, we've got no money, so you might as well stop wasting your time.'

In an instant, the rep who had shown us round and taken so much interest in our personal lives no longer wanted to be our best buddy. Amid lots of huffing and puffing we were awarded our bottle of cheap vodka and we then headed back to our apartment, on foot this time.

A few days later we met up with Mark again. He had now extended our plan to include a friend of his who was PR-ing for a different resort. We would get £25, Mark would get £10 and his mate would get £15 if we agreed to be sent by him to another resort.

We repeated this exercise three more times until we were caught out, having pocketed £125 in the process. What we hadn't banked on was one of the timeshare reps swapping resorts, and although there are dozens of salespeople working at each location, bad timing ensured we were hooked up with someone who had shown us around a different resort only a few days earlier.

'Don't I know you two?' he said as soon as he saw us. Naturally we denied it, but we were refused a tour and subsequent bottle of spirits and knew our game was up. However, we had acquired a pocketful of cash and a stash of vodka and, most importantly, we'd managed to survive five tours without actually buying a timeshare week.

The majority of couples from the street do escape without signing their finances away, but many of those who fall for it emerge bewildered and blinking into the daylight. They can't quite believe they're now owners of a 'property' in Tenerife that they can enjoy whenever they feel like escaping the UK for a dose of sub-tropical sunshine – as long as it's the second week in February and hefty management fees are paid.

'You'll be seeing a lot more of us from now on,' they'd boast over the bar top. 'We've just bought an apartment over there.'

'Congratulations. Owners, eh? You'll be asking for resident's discount next,' we'd joke. 'Is it timeshare?'

'Well… yes. It's like owning your own place though, isn't it?'

'Hmm,' we'd nod, polishing glasses knowingly.

Despite loathing the sales techniques, David and I decided that the timeshare intake would very likely be our next best bread and butter and so we were very wary about bad-mouthing the timeshare concept to customers. If they were daft enough to sign away thousands of pounds to commit themselves to the same week every year, who were we to dampen their enthusiasm? We'd already fallen into the trap of being many things to many people – marriage guidance counsellors, babysitters, life coaches and the rest – and we didn't want to add to our burden by becoming financial advisers as well.

Mindful of our need to cosy up with the timeshare companies, we offered to host fly-buy welcome meetings in the bar for a variety of different nationalities, in addition to the English-speaking contingent. In return for us laying on free jugs of sangria and a few bowls of ready salted, the timeshare reps would plug our food, entertainment and hospitality while Joy went about befriending as many of the welcome meeting attendees as she could get round in an hour. It meant having the bar ready an hour earlier every Friday, Saturday and Sunday morning, but it proved to be a fruitful effort. Many of the thirty or so people that had been enticed to each meeting would order breakfast or lunch, depending on how long they carried on drinking, and many would become regular patrons during the week. A lot of the timeshare reps also carried on drinking, often having to be helped back to their Altamira apartments by the very people they were trying to cajole into parting with a hefty sum of cash.

Admittedly, fly-buys amounted to only around half the number of customers that Airtours used to bring in, but we still had our resident patrons and actual apartment owners and the increase in takings meant we could at least pay the bills.

While some of the Friday fly-buy arrivals weren't the brightest crayons in the box, more than one or two of the timeshare workers exhibited a raft of personality disorders ranging from compulsive liar to delusions of grandeur. One such character was Burt, a tall and swarthy gent of German descent who sported the kind of moustache that ladies swooned over in the late 80s. Burt was a Lufthansa airline pilot, on a break. Or so he said. He shared a one-bedroom apartment with another timeshare pedlar in the fishing village of La Caleta. The apartment was lovely, with the ocean all but lapping at the flaking blue front door.

Many things didn't stack up in his version of his life story. On Monday he would tell us he was married with two children, and would proudly produce a wallet photo as proof. By Tuesday he would insist he was single, had never been married and never intended to get married. Wednesday would see a return to tales of his airline exploits, Thursday he'd tell us he'd been travelling the world for the past few years and on Friday he'd be back to the story about living in England with his wife and two kids. The tales would stop at the weekend, mainly because they were his days off and the amount of alcohol consumed rendered any conversation futile.

Burt was a prime example of how Tenerife gained one of its nicknames: Fantasy Island. A remote rock where anybody could reinvent themselves according to their own personal fantasies. We'd seen many who took advantage of this, including one man in the bar who'd insisted he was the director of a new five-star hotel in Las Américas, pointing to the emblazoned hotel slippers on his feet as evidence.

However, we grew to like Burt, irrespective of his previous life/lives. He was polite, kind and intelligent – a combination of traits that was hard to find in a British bar abroad in the mid 1990s. And because of our friendship and cooperation with Burt and the other timeshare wallahs, we were managing to keep our heads above water – just.

Chapter Sixteen

After that summer, the Smugglers did get noticeably quieter in the wake of the Airtours pull-out, despite our buddying up with the timeshare crowd. From doing 140 meals per night, the tally slipped to around sixty or seventy. While this was a cause for alarm on the accounting front, we remained hopeful that the vacuum would eventually be filled by another tour operator.

In the meantime, the reduction in workload gave us the opportunity to make a few improvements in the bar. Despite Frank's record of spectacular failures in the DIY department, we awarded him the job of redecorating.

The interior was looking decidedly shabby after years of nicotine clouds, fly poop, children's handprints, dust and general neglect. It was time for a freshen-up and change of colour, something cool, tropical and with decidedly more character than the 'smudged white' effect that we had now.

A refreshing pale 'mint green' was selected from a swatch that Frank had commandeered from a paint shop in Los Cristianos.

'Green?' huffed Frank. 'You want green? It'll look like a friggin' hospital.'

'It's tropical, but not too leafy,' I said helpfully.

'Medical, more like. Still, don't say I didn't warn you.' He duly noted the colour and sloped off in pursuit of 16 litres.

That night, after the last customers left at two in the morning, we began removing the fishing nets, decorative wine bottles and tarnished horse brasses from the walls. It was close to four o'clock when David, Joy and I stepped out into the warm night air, leaving a ghostly bar sketched with the dusty silhouettes of missing ornaments. Frank and his son, Danny, had muttered promises that they would have the bar painted and ready again by noon.

At 9am, bleary eyed and even more sleep deprived than normal, David, Joy and I headed off to Santa Cruz on yet another mission to apply for a work permit for Joy. The laws had recently been relaxed, which meant it was no longer compulsory to employ at least one Canarian before you could start employing immigrants such as ourselves.

If successful, and we knew it was a big if, this latest venture up north would make a huge difference. Not least, it would alleviate one more source of stress – the need for extra vigilance whenever a smartly dressed stranger walked into the bar. When this happened, we immediately had to bring Plan C(ustomer) into action. Either David or I would hiss 'Inspector!' at Joy. She'd then offload any plates, glasses or order books she was carrying, plonk herself at the nearest table, ignore the beckoning from every other table and look as casual as possible while perspiring profusely.

And why? So far, only David and I had managed to become fully legal. Originally our adviser had devised a cunning plan that would enable all of us to be legal straight away; this involved David marrying Faith, which he did, and Joy and me tying the knot, which we didn't. However, a few months after our arrival, the laws changed yet again and it then transpired that David's hastily arranged wedding had been futile anyway, in as much as this no longer provided a way of automatically being granted work permits.

Consequently, the only alternative was for David to be legally named as owner and for me, as a blood relative, to then become a full-time worker. But Joy had to remain on a ten-hours-per-week part-time contract until the bungling bureaucratic system stretched its legs again. If she was caught working longer than the contracted time, or outside the specific hours stipulated in the paperwork, we'd all be in serious trouble. Naturally this left Joy feeling a little left out and although in our eyes we were all equal partners, she couldn't help believing that she was lower status.

Aside from the psychological impact of this inequality, the practicalities of Plan C were also not great, as you can imagine. We were having to put it into action more and more often, thanks to the growing number of smartly dressed Jehovah's Witnesses who had decided to use our bar as a courage-building drinking point before embarking on their door-knocking crusade.

Although we were looking forward to putting the plan to bed once and for all, we were certainly not looking forward to our visit to the Department of Interminable Paperwork. There was only one lady who dealt with foreigners on this issue – the notorious Black Witch, feared by all the island's British expats who harboured dreams of one day becoming legal. The Black Witch was the gatekeeper for the holy work permit, and without her say-so you were doomed to endure clandestine employment forever.

The mood was low as David, Joy and I sped 50

165

miles up the TF-1 motorway linking the south with Santa Cruz in the north. Although a coastal road, you could hardly have called it scenic. As soon as Guaza Mountain and Los Cristianos had become mere specks in the rear-view mirror, the landscape turned to dust and desolation, littered with the odd storage depot, vehicle compound, builder's yard and neglected banana plantation.

The one-street town of Guaza was a taste of towns to come. Square blocks of flaking plaster housed an inordinate number of car showrooms where sullen salesmen sat picking their nails or flicking through auto magazines, yearning for cars that promised lives more exciting than their own.

David and I had experienced their overwhelming indifference first-hand. During a period of relative prosperity, and encouraged by a combination of boredom, decadence and aspiration, we decided to upgrade our battered Renault Express for something with a little more panache. Guaza had been our first point of call, given its healthy selection of car showrooms.

We entered the toilet-cubicle-sized office of a Peugeot dealer. 'We're looking for a new car, something with four doors, a lot of space and…'

A stick figure in his early twenties wearing a cheap grey suit two sizes too large sat in a black leather chair also two sizes too large, fiddling with a Rubik's cube. It was obvious he wasn't listening.

I reached behind and knocked loudly on the door we'd just come through. '*Hola.*'

The young man looked up and reluctantly removed an earphone from one side of his curly black mop. He flicked his chin up in a manner peculiar to Canarians, the opposite of the head-nod acknowledgement used by Brits.

'We want to buy a new car,' said David in his best Spanish.

The man shooed us out of his office with an index finger. 'They're out there,' he said in a tone that suggested we were complete imbeciles for not noticing the big shiny things with wheels that we had passed on the way in.

'I know—' I continued, but he had plugged both ears again and returned to frowning at the puzzle in his hands.

The young man who greeted us at the Volkswagen showroom eyed us suspiciously from a distance. We stood by the side of a gleaming black Golf TDI, stroking its roof like you'd pet a friendly dog. We made exaggerated noises of appreciation. We smiled at the frowning salesman and even beckoned him with a flick of the head, but it seemed nothing would persuade him to venture from the doorway of his office, not even the prospect of a sale.

We hoped for better service in the showroom next door. A Mitsubishi Shogun took our fancy, and in the absence of anybody trying to stop us, David and I climbed in and began our technical inspection. We checked all the major points of interest such as how many buttons and lights were on the dashboard, how comfortable the arm rest was and whether there was one of those fancy cup-holders that folded itself away when not in use. There was. We sat in awe, taking it in turns to audition its smooth movement and both nodded silently in appreciation. This was the car for us, but only if we could find somebody to sort out the financial arrangements.

Still sitting in the car, we looked around for signs of life in the showroom, but there were none. I opened and closed the door with a mighty thunk, but nobody came. David tried the horn, which though pleasing in its volume still didn't achieve the desired effect. After a couple more minutes we reluctantly got out, gazed at the big silver jeep wistfully and ambled off to yet another showroom, clinging to the faint hope that we might actually be able to buy a car from this one. But alas, it was not to be.

As with every task in Tenerife, it seemed that purchasing a vehicle was just too much like hard work for both the buyer and the seller. However, we were forced into reprising our quest when the Renault Express developed narcolepsy, falling asleep at the most inopportune moments, such as on busy roundabouts and in motorway fast lanes, and finally when driving into the car showroom at the point of part-exchange. Thankfully the Jeep salesperson was preoccupied at the time (naturally), so we pushed the Renault onto a down ramp and free-wheeled it to a stop outside the showroom, successfully saving a fair chunk of money in a part-exchange deal.

Needless to say, our experience in Guaza left us with a tarnished image of a town dogged by unfriendly slovenliness, an image that pertains to this day.

As you slog further along the TF-1, the next notable conurbation is Las Chafiras, baring a motley array of warehouse frontage to all that pass along the motorway. To be fair, industrial Las Chafiras wasn't developed to elicit whoops of delight for its aesthetics, which is just as well as it's about as attractive as a hog in high heels. It's the ugly end of brands such as Coca-Cola, Kalise ice creams and Dorada beer.

Understandably, such landmarks don't exactly raise the spirits of people like us trucking up to Santa Cruz to do battle with bureaucracy. In fact the entire TF-1 corridor seems to have been bestowed with such ugliness that by the time you confront the mistress of your fate, the will to live, let alone fight, has been all but snuffed out. We certainly felt like that after we'd negotiated the last of the three bends on the TF-1, all of which feature a camber more often found in amusement parks, a leaning curvature that sends any vehicle travelling at more than 50mph into a graceful but panicky drift towards the crash barriers.

By the time we'd found a parking space in a city that boasted just three, had creaked open the doors of the Ministry of Work and Social Security and had taken our places at the back of a very long line of similarly suicidal foreigners, we had as much enthusiasm for life as a trio of Siberian salt mine prisoners.

The traditional ticketed queuing system was in place so I pulled on a stub that poked from a round red container. The roll of tickets must have been near the end as the whole darn coil quickly unfurled out of the box and heaped itself into an unkempt pile on the floor, leaving me clutching ticket numbers 402, 403, 404 and so on, right up to 499.

A hundred faces turned to stare as I tried to fold

the mess neatly back into some kind of order, then dropped them all and stepped away quickly as a security guard scurried over with one hand menacingly on his baton. I smiled apologetically, which seemed to work. Instead of beating me about the head with a length of reinforced rubber, he tutted loudly, gathered up the pile in his arms and took it to his little plastic chair in the corner where, with tongue protruding from one side of his mouth, he folded the tickets one by one, with all the loving attention of a grandmother knitting socks for a new-born.

After a few days the queue shortened and we were at the front. Finally the door to the Black Witch's office opened and a beleaguered man scuttled out, shedding paperwork from manila folders with every step. A booming voice from within the room echoed along the corridor where we were all waiting, presumably hurling abuse and instructions at the poor man, who was now fumbling at the main door in a bid to escape.

As penance for having royally cocked up the queuing system, the security guard made David, Joy and me enter the coven together with the two couples standing behind us. The cavernous room was occupied by a solitary desk at the far end of an expanse of white tiles. Behind the desk sat one person, who, as her nickname suggested, appeared to be black in all but skin. She eyed our crowd from beneath a sharply cut fringe of dyed black. Black fingernails drummed impatiently on one of several tall sheaves of paper as tentatively we all approached like characters meeting 'the great and powerful' in *The Wizard of Oz*. If Joy was Dorothy, all front and bravado, I most certainly was the Lion, following in her footsteps full of fear and trepidation.

There were only three chairs to accommodate our party of seven. The Black Witch, impatient with our dallying over who should have the seats, coughed loudly and Joy and the two other women sat down quickly.

She held out her hands for paperwork. David handed Joy our wad, which was dutifully passed over. A tall man with a pallid complexion – we'll call him the Tin Man – leaned over his wife and passed his papers. While this was happening, I could see the woman sitting in the middle, who had unkempt, scarecrow hair, rummaging in the Corte Ingles shopping bag at her feet. Instead of application forms, she emerged from the bag with a box of Lindt chocolates, which she placed in the hands of the Black Witch.

I looked at David, Joy looked at the Scarecrow and the Black Witch looked at the box of chocolates. She broke into a half smile, like a vampire viewing garlic.

'*Salud*,' she mumbled. Cheers.

'What did she say?' whispered Scarecrow, craning round to her husband.

'I think she wants us to salute,' he hissed back and urgently beckoned her to stand up.

The rest of us watched, bewildered, as the couple stood to attention and saluted with military precision. The Black Witch blinked, expressionless, slowly shook her head, then one by one dismissed all our applications for various reasons, including bribery (Scarecrow), vandalism (me) and simply because she could (the other couple). It would take two further visits before Joy was finally granted full legal status and the right not to have to sit down whenever a Jehovah's Witness stopped by for a pint.

~

Our disappointment that a miracle hadn't happened regarding our paperwork being accepted first time around was tempered by our curiosity about how the newly decorated bar would look when we got back. Frank had done many DIY jobs for us, most of which had ended in disaster, but he was cheap, would work flexible hours and was keen to turn his hand to anything that we needed doing.

As it turned out, while he had been spectacularly misguided in removing the safety valve from our gas cabinet, and appallingly incorrect in his assumption that we wouldn't mind having to employ a golf club to extract water from our kitchen taps, he was actually right when it came to advising against our chosen colour scheme for the bar.

'Holy crap,' said David when we opened the Smugglers door.

'What the hell...?' added Joy.

'Oh shit,' I said.

The walls were snot green. Instead of a refreshing minty tint, the inside of the Smugglers resembled either deep jungle or interior nostril, depending on how much light fell on the walls through the glass frontage.

'It's... different,' I offered.

'It's horrible,' said David.

'It's not staying like that!' said Joy.

In addition to sporting a proud told-you-so smirk, Frank was now also sporting an extra lump of cash as we employed him to dampen down the Amazonian look with a coat of pale cream. However, the refreshing minty tint remained elusive and the layers of colour, together with Frank's excessive watering down, meant we were left with nothing more appealing than a marbled mould effect.

JOE CAWLEY

Chapter Seventeen

As well as allowing space to make some much-needed improvements, the drop in custom also afforded us the luxury of a little more leisure time to have some fun, and get fit. The seven-days-a-week drinking routine was leaving its mark.

It was hard not to drink when you owned and worked in a bar. Apart from the actual desire to submerge any stress in a pint of alcohol, there were continual offers of 'drinks for the lads in the kitchen' or 'and one for yourself'. The first thing that was needed when you'd just spent six draining hours in the 140-degree furnace of the kitchen was a cooling beer, which inevitably was downed in a matter of seconds. And the easiest way to conceal the exhaustion and desire to lie down was to quickly get as drunk as those in your immediate surroundings, all of whom would have had several hours' head start.

Needless to say, waistbands had expanded, jowls had become baggy and energy levels had sagged. Sport was the answer, and with this in mind David and I set about attaching a satellite TV dish to the roof of the empty *local* next door. Well, it was a start.

''Scuse me, chaps.' David and I were tightening the last bolts when Roger, president of the El Beril community, shouted from below.

By law, every complex in Tenerife has to have a community organisation, headed by an elected president who ensures that both community and regional laws are respected and that the interests of the community are well served. This was Roger's fifth term as president, an extraordinary length of office given that it was a role that few wanted to take on. And who could blame them? I mean, why buy a relaxing holiday home in the sun and then set yourself up to be the object of derision, hate and even aggression in some cases? It made no sense to me, but Roger thrived in the role, 'reluctantly' accepting the responsibility at every Annual General Meeting due to a lack of other volunteer candidates.

'What in hell's name are you doing?' he bellowed.

David and I looked at each other. 'It's a satellite dish,' said David.

'Yes, I can see that. But you can't strap sodding great satellite dishes willy-nilly all over the place. You need permission from the community.' He scribbled a note on the clipboard he was carrying.

'How do we get that?' I asked.

'You ask me, the president,' said Roger.

'Oh. Okay. So, can we put a satellite dish up here?'

'No… No, you bloody well can't. For one thing that's not your *local*, and besides that, if I let everybody put dishes up, this place would look like Jodrell Bank in two weeks.'

'We need it for the bar,' I said. 'Every bar's getting one. If *we* don't, all our customers will go elsewhere to watch the football…'

'… and rugby,' added David quickly.

'Rugby?' Roger unfolded his arms. 'You can get rugby on it?'

'All the big games,' said David. 'Live.'

'League or Union?'

'Both.'

'Five Nations?'

'Yep.'

He tapped his nose. 'I've not seen you. Carry on, chaps.' And with that, he walked off, shielding his view of us with his clipboard.

It was true that the satellite system was for the bar, but David and I had our own interests in mind. Keen Man United supporters since our dad had introduced us to the skills of Willie Morgan et al at Old Trafford, we were ecstatic to have a viable reason for investing what was a hefty sum for access to live English football.

As with many grown-up boys, the very thought of match day action conjured notions of being able to kick a ball around with the same poise and style as our sporting heroes. One thing quickly led to another and without sensibly thinking the whole idea through, we had organised the very first Smugglers five-a-side match.

The opposing team consisted of five young brothers from Oldham who had come on holiday with their parents and girlfriends. Two of them played for Tranmere Rovers' youth team, one was having trials with Everton and the other two had represented England at junior level.

Our team consisted of two brothers who reasoned that being able to set up *and* tune in Sky Sports on a satellite box all by themselves would compensate for a lack of ball skills; Barry, our quizmaster, who was immediately signed up after he boasted that he'd once refereed a police football match; Frank, who at fifty-one was the third youngest member of our team and had agreed to

177

join on the promise of free post-match beer; and Mike, an ex-army officer from Northern Ireland, who at one time in his life must have been a great deal fitter than his sagging belly now suggested.

We also had a few 'secret weapons' on the bench. One was Burt the German timeshare salesman, who, since we'd mentioned the match, had added the title of goalkeeper for Borussia Mönchengladbach to his varied range of previous careers.

Another back-up was Wayne, our pot-smoking friend from Birmingham, who had returned for an autumn of sunshine and beaming contentment at the business end of a doobie. 'Us'll play, no problem,' he had said, sucking in a lungful of herb infusion, then adding a few moments later as he blew the smoke out, 'Erm... play what?'

So, with our formidable Smugglers football team packed into the back of our new Jeep Cherokee, we headed down to Los Cristianos sports centre for a 7pm kick-off.

The huge hall seemed even larger whenever we were prompted to pass a ball from one end to the other. My attempt to float one on to David's head feebly rolled across a succession of coloured lines then petered out at the halfway line. Trainers – or, in Wayne's case, Doc Martins –squeaked as the seven of us started to loosen up before the other team arrived.

'Okay, we warm up,' commanded Burt, beckoning us to follow him and his groin-length white shorts on a lap round the playing area.

No sooner had we started than Barry cried out. 'Ow, ow!' He stumbled across the pitch to the benches, holding on to the back of his thigh. 'That's me done, boys. Pulled something in me leg.'

Burt continued leading the six of us on a second lap of the pitch. Although the hall was well equipped with lines of various colour and notices that spelled out any number of sporting regulations, what it did lack was an adequate supply of breathable air. My eyes stung as beads of sweat rolled from forehead to floor, lungs scrambling to replace oxygen with a musky alternative of body odour, dust and the smell of Mike's fetid trainers.

'Sod that for a game of soldiers,' said Wayne. He joined Barry on the bench and set about rolling a joint. The rest of us stopped trailing Burt, leaving him to jog on, oblivious to the rebellion.

The other team arrived and began to pass and shoot with a skill and accuracy that was as mesmerising as it was disconcerting. We decided to take it in turns to be goalkeeper, swapping every time we conceded. Ten minutes into the first half, I grabbed the gloves from Mike for my second stint as cannon fodder. At 5–0 down and without a shot on target, any hope of a victorious return to the bar had been mercilessly crushed.

David had joined Barry on the bench after only his second kick, twisting an ankle after a spectacular shot that had he actually connected with the ball would have been hard to stop. Wayne came on as sub, and although his limbs were intact, his brain unfortunately wasn't. He spent the whole match in the centre circle, watching play go on around him, chuckling randomly.

Needless to say, we lost – if 37–1 still counts as a loss and not all-out decimation. Mike was the hero behind our only goal after a clearance from their goalie ricocheted in off the back of his head while he was remonstrating with Wayne.

Still, it had proven a success in providing a distraction and reminding us how unfit we all were, and it had made David and me realise that playing football was nowhere near as pleasurable as watching it in your own bar with free beer on tap.

~

Being able to show live football did bring in a few extra patrons, but as most were so engrossed in watching the action, the rate of beer consumption was not enough to even cover the costs of the system and our cash flow continued to be tight. To make matters worse, access to Las Américas and the rest of civilisation was getting easier by the month, with new roads, new coastal paths and the launching of a bus route from the top of the El Beril road.

To keep tabs on our outgoings, we were still using the envelope accounting system that we had initiated when we'd started at the bar. This entailed stuffing a dozen or so envelopes with bundles of cash at the end of each night to try and ensure we could cover the bills for the electricity, water and tax, and the wages of Sammy and the army of other beneficiaries that sucked the profit out of the Smugglers. However, as the cash got tighter, the accounting became more of a juggling act, swapping notes from one envelope to another as the bills came thick and fast.

The two nights of the year that we could rely on

were Christmas Day and New Year's Eve. No matter how little or how much we took through the year, these two days were consistently munificent, especially the latter. Although summer saw an intensive flurry of holiday arrivals in July and August, Tenerife was still known as the winter sun destination and received the most visitors when the face of northern Europe turned pallid.

Those who chose to splash out on celebrating Christmas and New Year in the sub-tropical sunshine were the sort most likely to let loose with both cannons of their spending power. Thus the relatively high price tag we put on Christmas dinner and New Year drinks was generally accepted without fuss, boosting the bar takings for the year by a considerable amount.

If we were to survive into our sixth year of trading, the coming festive season would need to elicit one of the best and biggest takings yet. All thoughts were focused on planning the meal and entertainment and maximising the space to fit in as many covers as we could without clients having to virtually sit on each other's laps.

As in previous years, our full-time festive-period staff had been boosted by one – namely Cousin Les, the youngest of our five cousins. He had flown over for his fifth Christmas with us, having finished his studies in music and drama. More a fan of tinsel than turkey, Cousin Les saw the Christmas job in Tenerife as both a sunny escape from the traditional family gathering and an opportunity to acquire a healthy glow that would do him no harm in the gay saunas back in Leeds.

For our part, the Smugglers gained an additional

pair of hands when we most needed it, David gained live-in company over the holiday season, and we no longer had to waste money on the usual miscreants that we foolishly employed under the misguided assumption that many hands made light work. Best of all, Cousin Les was the ideal working partner, liable to burst into song and dance at any given moment. His sharp wit and occasional mincing provided a welcome deluge of positivity at a point when our catering careers were suffering a serious drought of fun.

On a fleeting visit to Tenerife six months earlier, during the summer of 1996, Cousin Les had brought company. 'This is Andi,' he'd said as David, Joy and I sat at the bar flicking cockroaches at the spirit bottles. David fumbled for a cigarette and started smoking out of the side of his mouth. Joy and I exchanged knowing glances. It transpired that Andi, or Andrea, to give her her full title, had been a fellow student of Les's at Leeds. She had an elf-like figure and eyes that sparkled with joie de vivre even though she'd recently split from a long-term boyfriend. Sheltering under the comforting wing of Cousin Les, she had bought his theory that 'out of sight, out of mind' was the therapy she needed and had tagged along on his summer foray to the sub-tropics. It soon became clear that she was just as exuberant as Cousin Les and she began to brighten our despondence considerably. Especially, as it turned out, David's.

Towards the end of the two-week summer break the trio became a duo as David and Andi developed a relationship that bore no resemblance whatsoever to his previous casual flings with holidaymakers.

Those usually ended with David hiding in the bar while a heartbroken holidaymaker dragged her suitcase around El Beril in a desperate bid to find him before boarding the coach to the airport. Joy in particular was often at the soggy end of proclamations of undying love featuring vows to 'phone David every day' and messages such as, 'You will tell him I love him, won't you?'

Holiday relationships are strange things. From behind the bar we saw many. Strangers from different parts of the world converged on our little patch of 'paradise' for a fortnight of sun, sand and sea, then added a further 's' as hot nights, exposed flesh on the beaches and a feeling of transiency in a foreign land thousands of miles from conscience, responsibility and reality led to a holiday fling.

We'd witnessed the one-sided affairs where the girl (usually) falls madly and deeply in love, assuming reciprocal love and devotion when in fact the bloke is quite happy with getting his leg over then moving right along, thank you very much. We'd also seen the reverse, but not quite so often, it has to be said. Holiday and timeshare reps were notorious for this, considering a succession of no-obligation bed buddies as a perk of the job.

We'd also been privy to holiday relationships with a happier ending, where that super-charged emotion coursing through the veins of both parties continued long after rubber left tarmac on the Tenerife South runway. To date we'd seen at least one long-lasting relationship formed every year, a smitten couple returning the following year to bask in the birthplace of what had now become a permanent union.

At first, Joy and I weren't too sure what to make of David and Andi's relationship. We'd seen him sink a few hearts previously, falsifying his feelings with the holidaying girl to maximise the experience. But this time it was different. I knew it was serious – I was very astute like that. Subtle clues such as Andi returning to Tenerife six times throughout the second half of 1996 and David heading back to the UK twice in the same year were seized upon and used to confront my brother about the depth of his feelings. He was smitten.

By the winter of 1996, although the thermometer registered a drop in temperature from summer highs of 36 to November highs of 26, the heat had most certainly been turned up in David and Andi's relationship. Early in December Andi moved over, and quite sensibly found employment outside of the Smugglers, managing a car rental office next to Bar Arancha on the floor above. The hours were nine till one, and then four till seven, following which, more often than not, she'd lend a hand in the bar during the run-up to Christmas.

Despite our best efforts, the arrival of the cavalry in the form of Cousin Les and Andi, and the soulful warbling of our perennial favourite artist, Gene Alexander, the uptake of reservations for Christmas Day at the Smugglers that year was poor. We had struggled to fill all seventy-two places inside and had sold none of the outside tables, mainly because the preceding week had been unseasonably dull and chilly. The day came and went as smoothly as it could have done, which was a damn sight more smoothly than the first couple of Christmas disasters involving frozen turkeys, drunken revellers and toppling trees.

But there were just not enough people to make up for the poor summer. All hopes of survival were now pinned on having the busiest New Year's Eve ever. If we didn't, quite simply we wouldn't be able to cover the next few months of mortgage and loan repayments.

Despite the disappointing Christmas turnout, we kept all guns blazing leading up to the big 1996 New Year's Eve Party. David had gone manic with the fluorescent highlighter pens, Joy was promoting the 'best night in Tenerife' to anybody who would listen as well as many that wouldn't, and I was pushing leaflets under every door in the Altamira and El Beril, as well as stuffing them under the windscreen wipers of every vehicle in a half-mile radius.

The envelopes had been raided so we could buy extra stock and decorations and even hire a few small disco lights. We were working twenty-hour days to make sure everything was ready. Shopping, food preparation and marketing efforts were squeezed in between bar shifts and by the morning of December 30th we had everything in place. Patrons promised that they'd see in 1997 at the Smugglers. And then, not for the first time in our Smugglers careers, disaster struck.

JOE CAWLEY

EVEN MORE KETCHUP THAN SALSA

Chapter Eighteen

The day had started as normally as any other day in 'Paradise', except that today was December 30th, the day before New Year's Eve. We'd had our usual array of customers – from the dedicated to the demented. Friedhelm, our loyal German patron, had spent most of the morning in the Smugglers sobbing into a succession of frothy pints. For a sizeable number of single seniors, the festive period merely fanned the flames of despair and loneliness, and Friedhelm was no exception. Joy had tried on several occasions to fathom out the specific depths of Friedhelm's misery, but her sympathetic enquiries merely exacerbated the wailing so she gave up.

The self-proclaimed King of the Canary Islands had made a dramatic return. We hadn't seen Johan for several months and I'd missed the unpredictability he brought, this insane, twenty-six-year-old German dropout with his over-indulgence in recreational drugs and his penchant for Broadway musicals. No doubt he'd been busy with majestic matters in his wigwam palace on Spaghetti Beach at the far side of La Caleta.

Resplendent in his royal attire of plastic-water-bottle crown and black-bin-liner robe, he flounced into the bar, tied an imaginary horse to the beer pump and with hands on hips announced to a bar full of baffled breakfast munchers that he cleared the island of dragons and we needn't live in fear a moment longer. The diners presumably took heed, and continued gorging on Heinz beans and buttered slices of Warburton's.

Joy was leading him out by his arm when suddenly he spotted a gecko sunbathing on the whitewashed wall outside. He leapt back up the stairs, shouting, 'They're back! They're back! Run for your lives!' as the tiny lizard scuttled for sanctuary in a crack in the wall. Ten minutes later he returned, mumbled feebly, 'Forgot my horse,' and untied his imaginary companion from the beer pump and led it away.

We'd all become inured to the madcap antics of both expat eccentrics and the local crazies, rarely bothering to lift our heads when the latest episode of surrealism surfaced. However, behaviour that put our livelihood under threat, and in particular behaviour that threatened to have our livelihood literally go up in smoke, couldn't be ignored.

~

'Erm… I think you'd better come. There's been an… occurrence. ' Cousin Les was trying to be calm as he stood in the doorway of Number 85. 'Come on,' he urged. 'Something has gone a bit Pete Tong in the kitchen.' The words were audible but bounced off my brain without leaving an impression.

'Quick, the pissing bar's on fire!' he continued, trying to inject a little more haste into the proceedings.

I was dressed in nothing but boxer shorts and a lop-sided hairstyle befitting someone who had been rudely awakened from a much-needed afternoon siesta. Gradually, the wheels of comprehension started to gain momentum.

'Shit,' I said, before racing back into the bedroom and trying to squeeze into a pair of Joy's cut-off jeans and an inside-out Smugglers Tavern T-shirt. Joy was still in bed, cocooned in white cotton from toes to chin.

'Joy,' I whispered. 'Think you'd better get up.'

'Who is it?' she mumbled, eyes still closed.

'Cousin Les… says the bar's on fire.'

Her eyes sprang open a second before she leapt out of bed, grabbing whatever clothes were at hand. Within sixty seconds we were sprinting through the El Beril complex.

A crowd had gathered alongside the top railings, watching the funnel of thick black smoke pouring from the bar door and smothering the bright blue sky in a dusty veil of mourning. Cousin Les stood outside frantically wafting the billowing smoke with a plastic spatula. David emerged from the bar, removed a Dorada beer towel from his nose and mouth and gasped for air. Cousin Les turned his wafting to David.

'What happened?' I said, coughing as the acrid smoke filled my lungs. Cousin Les turned to waft me.

'The… the oven… it caught fire,' spluttered David between bouts of coughing. Cousin Les began alternating his spatula waving between the two of us.

'Cousin Les! Will you put that soddin' spatula down,' I shouted. 'Are you okay, bruv?'

David nodded. 'Think it's out now,' he coughed.

'Has anyone called the fire brigade?' A distant siren answered Joy's enquiry.

By now the upper level was full of peering faces. They watched as La Caleta's volunteer fire service dragged a hose through the crowd, down the steps and straight into Patricia's supermarket next door.

Cousin Les and I looked at each other quizzically.

'*Aquí! Aquí!*' yelled Cousin Les at the last of their number. (Over here! Over here!)

'Where the smoke is!' I added plaintively and pointed at the billowing plumes.

The last fireman shouted to his colleagues. One by one, Cuthbert, Dibble and Grub rushed out of the supermarket and ran into the bar. David and I followed. The smoke had begun to thin, revealing an interior swathed in ash and soot. The once white tiles at the far side of the kitchen were now completely black, the extractor hood buckled by the heat. Every surface was ash black, from floor to ceiling.

As we surveyed the devastation, the front fireman suddenly let loose with a cannon of foam, spraying in every direction. 'It's out! It's out!' we shouted, waving at them to stop, but to no avail. They had a foam hose and they were damn well going to use it. When they'd doused the kitchen with a satisfactory amount of bubbles, the firemen turned their attention to the cushioned bench seats, the glass-topped tables, the shelf of empty wine bottles lining the entire perimeter, the blackened Christmas tree that we'd kidnapped from the mountains, the mirrored spirit shelf, and just for good measure all the CD players and satellite boxes, plus the expensive PA and lighting system that we had safely stacked away from harm's reach behind the bar.

When they'd finished, we followed them out, eyes streaming from the smoke. Joy was still standing outside, not daring to view the damage. 'How bad is it?' she asked. It was December 30th. Tomorrow night was to have been our saving grace. A New Year's Eve party that could potentially have put us back on track financially. How much worse could it be?

Joy shook the soot off an order book. 'It'll take weeks to clear this lot and open up again.'

'Well, I suppose it gives us a reason to give the bar a spring clean, now,' I said, trying to lighten the mood.

The firemen had reeled in their hoses and the crowd started to disperse. Several holidaymakers offered their condolences before turning their backs and heading for the beach.

'We need to completely empty it before we can start cleaning,' said David.

We all picked up whatever was closest to hand. In my case this was a box of melted party poppers and blowers for our New Year's Eve party.

'Won't be needing those now,' said Cousin Les, sagely.

I threw them in the bin along with other items that were either so badly damaged they were beyond saving, or that had no purpose and had been dust collectors for too long now: the electric meat slicer that had been banished to the naughty corner under the kitchen sink for maliciously carving off the tip of Joy's index finger in the early days; the jaunty ash-cloaked sign above the sink that read, 'Pots on the dryer, dishes in the sink, I'll leave it till tomorrow, right now I need a drink'; and the range of cocktail books behind the bar that since we'd become mix experts had served no other purpose than to house several generations of tiny cockroaches.

'Shall we save these for next year?' said David, holding up a bag of New Year's Eve bunting and other decorations that had avoided damage.

'Might as well,' said Cousin Les. 'We're not going to be using them this year.'

'We might not need them then either,' said Joy. 'I doubt we'll still be open by then.'

I removed the kitchen clock from the wall, blew ash off the face and noted that it was six o'clock – opening time. 'Do you think we should put a "Closed" notice on the door?'

'Erm, I think the blackened interior and foam everywhere might give the game away, don't you?' said Joy.

But just as she finished the sentence, the doors were pushed open and a smartly dressed couple we had served the night before poked their heads in.

'Oh!' they said, understating the severity of the situation in typical British manner. 'What happened?'

'We've had a fire,' said Joy.

'Oh,' they repeated, and retreated hastily.

It wasn't long before more hungry patrons appeared, dressed in neatly ironed holiday slacks and shirts. 'Had a fire?' several noted brightly, as if it was a common occurrence, like running out of ice.

Next to burst through the door was Justin, son of a high court judge and her executive husband.

The family owned an apartment in Altamira and spent months at a time in it, whenever work schedules would allow. Justin lived in a different world for most of his waking hours, highly intellectual but startlingly deficient in matters of common sense, and blissfully unaware of any dramas unfolding around him.

He sat at one of the tables for a couple of minutes, drumming his fingers on the blackened glass while gazing round through thick spectacles as if trying to work out what was different.

'Can I get myself a Coke, Joy?' he shouted from the table. We often let the kids help themselves to soft drinks from the Pepsi pump when we were all too busy. The cost was minimal but the novelty never waned and ensured that given the choice, the Smugglers was their (and therefore their parents') preferred watering hole.

'Sure, but it might be warm,' shouted Joy from the kitchen. 'The electric's off.'

I heard the sssshhh from the tap as he filled his glass. 'Shall I put the music on, Joy?'

'Err... no. The electric's off, Justin.'

'Oh... okay.'

'Do you want to help us in here, Justin?' shouted Cousin Les from the kitchen.

'Okay. Shall I put the lights on?'

'Electric?' shouted Joy, with just a little less patience this time.

Justin ambled into the kitchen, sloshing Coke all down what looked like a brand-new yellow T-shirt.

'How can you see in here?' he beamed. 'Why haven't you got the lights on?'

Cousin Les and Joy sighed and shook their heads

in resignation.

'Can I have a Hawaiian Burger, David?' David had his head in the oven, scrubbing the interior. I could hear him mumbling from within. 'No pineapple,' continued Justin. 'Or chicken. Can I have it with a hamburger in instead?'

I couldn't resist. 'Like a hamburger then?'

'No, a Hawaiian Burger,' he replied, with no sign of having understood.

'Justin, have you noticed anything different in here?' asked Joy calmly.

'Err, yes, it's darker than usual. Do you want me to put the lights on?'

'Forget the lights, Justin. We have no electricity. We have no electricity because the wires burnt out. And the wires burnt out because we've had a fire. Here. In the kitchen.'

'Oh,' he said. Then a moment later, 'Why?'

But before we had the chance to kill him, Justin's parents appeared. They took one look at our now blackened faces, turned round and strutted off without saying a word. Justin skipped after them. Charming, I thought. Abandoned in our hour of need. To our customers, the fire was just an inconvenience; to us, it spelt the end.

And then a remarkable thing happened. One by one, all the holidaymakers and residents that had popped their heads in and then made a hasty retreat started pouring through the doors. They had all gone back home, changed from going-out clothes into the scruffiest they could find, and returned to help.

'What can we do?' they asked. A crowd of around twenty faced the four of us as we peered out with blackened faces from the kitchen doorway. 'We're here to help.' From the beer monsters to the gin and tonic sippers, they'd sacrificed an evening of their holiday to get deep down and dirty helping us in our darkest hour.

Justin's dad quickly organised a chain gang to pass everything from inside onto the patio, where Sammy had arranged bowls of soapy water on one row of plastic tables and a pile of faded beer towels to use for drying on another.

Friedhelm came in, sat at his usual beer barrel and ordered a 'big beer', completely oblivious to the fuss around him. Obviously, having no electricity meant that the beer cooler didn't do anything of the sort, but rather than explain this, I poured him a pint of warm froth and took it to him. He took a noisy sip, leaving a tuft of white froth on the tip of his nose as he gazed around at all the activity.

Before long every long-forgotten bottle of spirits lurking on the mirrored shelves, every square glass tabletop and every jaunty maritime ornament had been transported into the open air, where it was scrubbed and left to dry on the pool table.

'I've cleaned the kettle, Joy,' said Marjorie, one of El Beril's regular winter residents.

Not surprisingly, the sight of well-to-do expats and holidaymakers cleaning dishes and glasses while dressed in Armani and Marigolds drew quite a crowd at the railings on the upper level. Russian and French timeshare owners looked on curiously, trying to figure out if this was some kind of organised entertainment that they were missing out on or just a bunch of barmy Brits being their eccentric selves again.

195

'Done the condiment sets, Joy,' shouted Marjorie again, waving a salt pot in the air and unwittingly adding a sprinkling of minerals to Sammy's golden locks.

'Thanks, Marj,' said Joy, without looking up.

While it was heart-warming to see some of our loyal holidaymakers and a handful of residents coming to our rescue, several people were notable not so much for their absence as for their avoidance. Frank, for one, had been bought by the enemy for the price of the odd bottle of free beer and now sat outside Tel's Bar nursing a chilled Dorada. I caught his eye as I helped David out with the kitchen table, but he quickly turned away, embarrassed.

Before long the blue sky paled then blushed from salmon pink to burnt orange and fiery red, the colour finally fading into a blanket of star-studded black.

We were all grimed in soot, grease and sweat, but still everybody worked on through the evening, fuelled by warm bottles of beer from the fridge and pizza delivered from Las Américas. Marjorie had now informed Joy about all seventeen items she'd personally cleaned, obviously keen to let everybody know that she'd done her bit in the battle. Justin had finally twigged that we'd had a fire and sat on the steps with his head cupped in his hands, watching his parents wash, dry and polish item after item.

We also had an untimely visit from the King of Tenerife who had 'ridden in' on his imaginary horse again.

'We've had a fire,' explained Joy.

'Who did this?' he demanded, drawing a bamboo-cane sword. 'I will find them and cut right off their head. Then I give it to you on a tea tray.'

'Okay, fair enough,' said Joy, too exhausted to contest his imaginary world.

But before riding off on his mission, the King took a seat beside Marjorie and joined in the clean-up. Marjorie hitched her round glasses further up the bridge of her nose and smiled nervously at her new cleaning partner.

'Evening, love,' she ventured.

'Aha, a princess… of untold beauty.'

Marjorie's hamster-like cheeks turned bright red.

In the kitchen four customers pulled the sofa-sized oven away from the wall so we could clean the tiles behind it.

'Blimey,' said Philip, a city financier. 'It's amazing what a mess that fire has made. Look at all the grease that's melted behind here.' We knew that the fire had nothing to do with that. The oven hadn't been pulled out since we took over five and a half years ago.

By midnight, Joy, David, Cousin Les, Andi and I were the only ones left. Miraculously, the interior was almost back to the same condition it had been in before the fire. In fact it was a damn sight cleaner in many places. If it hadn't been for the lingering smell of smoke, and walls still damp from exuberant foam-spraying, you'd have been forgiven for thinking that nothing major had happened. Although the fixtures, fittings and other portable objects were still outside, it began to dawn on us that the New Year's Eve Party might still be possible after all.

197

David, Cousin Les and I set about refurnishing the bar and kitchen while Joy and Andi made use of the half-dozen apartments for which we still held the keys, bundling the cushion covers, tablecloths and tea towels into their washing machines and stuffing our frozen food into their freezers.

Finally, at six in the morning, the bar was just about ready for business once again. All of the food in the fridges had naturally been ruined so one last job was to make a shopping list for everything we needed for the party. We opted for the luxury of four hours sleep, agreeing to rendezvous back at the bar at ten the following morning, when it would be all hands on deck to shop, decorate and generally prepare for what we still hoped would be the biggest night of the year. On top of that, we also had to make sure that everyone knew we would still be open for business, so a last-minute leaflet drop was arranged, with Andi putting the photocopier through its paces upstairs in the car hire office.

We were due to open at 7.30, which, by the time we'd completed all our assigned missions, gave us just half an hour to shower, change and muster whatever energy we could for the big night ahead. We were mentally and physically exhausted, but we couldn't allow that to affect the atmosphere. At 7.25, with a crowd starting to converge outside, we opened a bottle of champagne in the kitchen.

'To us, to the Smugglers, and to them,' said David, lifting a glass to the people staring in from outside.

'Restores your faith in humanity,' said Joy. 'Well, in most of them,' she added as we watched Justin bang his head on the glass as he tried to peer through the doors.

As for the takings… let's just say we didn't have time to replace the till roll after the first one ran out just before eleven. That very British 'trench' spirit pervaded the whole evening and for the first time in years there was a sense of the community pulling together. For this one night, no longer was it us and them, we were all in it together.

That didn't last long though.

JOE CAWLEY

EVEN MORE KETCHUP THAN SALSA

Chapter Nineteen

Horse Race nights were one of the few evening entertainments that we continued to put on, now we were catering for a more international clientele. For those who've never experienced the thrill of wasting your money on televised galloping, let me explain.

Behind the bar we kept a stack of VHS tapes, each showing a staged race between eight horses with the winner pre-determined. After showing the horses being led round the paddock, we'd pause the tape for customers to come to the bar and bet on who they thought was going to win – based on odds, age of horse and of course what colour shirt the jockey was sporting. The stakes were kept to a minimum – 250 pesetas per bet, the price of a pint of beer – but that didn't lessen the tension or the seriousness of the event and the decibels would explode as soon as the race started.

As usual, we had a bar packed mostly with Brits, but also a few Germans who miraculously understood Joy's mimed explanation involving whips, bending over and running the length of the bar whooping at an imaginary horse. I could tell from the glint in Friedhelm's eye that after watching Joy's actions horse racing was the last thing he was thinking of.

It was just at the end of race number four, the last race of a particularly raucous night, that proceedings went awry.

'*Ein grosses bier*?' I smiled at the silver-haired man perched at the end of the bar. I hadn't seen him before. He'd been sitting on his own for two races, slowly sipping frothy Dorada and smiling at the euphoria of the winners. He smiled back but waved a finger to decline a refill and patted his chest with an exaggerated grimace, suggesting he had heartburn or indigestion.

'And it's just been announced... there will be a steward's enquiry,' said the race commentator through speakers positioned in every corner. The German and I turned to look at the screen. 'It looks like Paul Oakenfold on Greystones might just get disqualified after all,' continued the tape. I turned back and raised my eyebrows at the German, or at least where he had been sitting, but he was gone. I figured he must have gone to the toilet, but Joy knew otherwise.

'Joe, Joe,' she hissed. 'Get round here quick.' The elderly German had toppled off his stool.

We squatted next to him amid a forest of legs. He had obviously knocked himself out and was sprawled on his back with his head resting between the high heels of a German lady at table seven. She was blithely enjoying a gin and lemon and the show of British eccentricity in the bar.

Joy slapped the fallen man lightly across the face. 'Wakey-wakey.' No response. She tugged on his arm.

'Wait,' I said. 'If he's injured it's best not to move him. Go to the Altamira reception and call an ambulance.'

'Do you think he's okay?' she asked. 'I mean, is he, you know... still alive?'

I held his wrist and felt for a pulse. My eyes widened. Nothing. Joy put a hand over her mouth. The excited chatter and laughter in the bar turned into a distant and incomprehensible buzz broken only by a loud cheer as the commentator announced horse number five had been declared the winner.

From our crouched position I could feel the shove of legs as people turned and moved towards the bar.

'Whoops, didn't see you down there.'

'You lost something?'

'While you're down there…'

Somebody knocked on the bar top. 'Service!'

I stood up. 'Won't be a minute,' I said to the grinning Geordie. 'Got a bit of a situation here.'

A barrage of voices from the bar came back at me:

'Never mind that, where's me winnings?'

'Anything to avoid paying out!'

'He's alright, he's just drunk. Let him sleep it off.'

'Erm… I think he's dead,' I said, trying to sound as calm as I could. I expected a mad rush as people exited in horror, but nothing of the sort happened.

'Well there's not much you can do then, is there?' said Geordie. 'Pay up.'

'Everybody's going to have to leave the bar so we can let the doctors see to him,' I said, now installed behind the bar again.

A queue of punters, two-deep, were waving winning tickets at me.

'Hey, excuse me, but we're going nowhere till you pay up, sunshine,' added a loud voice from a man in a Bolton Wanderers T-shirt who had stepped over the body to reach the bar.

'A man has just died. Right here. In this bar.

He's still lying under your feet and all you're bothered about are your winnings?'

'That might well be,' said Bolton. 'But what about our money?'

'Bring your tickets tomorrow, you'll all be paid then,' I said and shook my head in disgust.

The crowd were still shuffling out when the medics arrived and confirmed the man was dead. A heart attack, they suspected. I caught a glimpse of Geordie and Bolton shaking their heads at the inconvenient disturbance this selfish dead German had caused. My recently restored faith in humanity vanished in that second.

As most well-embedded expats will tell you, your respect for a certain breed of holidaymaker decreases in direct proportion to the amount of time you've spent in a holiday resort. It's not intentional, it's not considered and perhaps it's unfair, but that's how it is. The locals called them *guiris*, the Brits in Tenerife call them Billies.

Billies ask the same questions day after day: 'How long have you been here?', 'Do you like it here?', 'Do you think you'll ever move back?' All sensible questions the first time you hear them, but unfortunately very irritating when you get asked them dozens of times every single day.

Billies want nothing more than Britain in the sun. They have no interest in Canarian culture, no desire to mix with Canarians, and a deep suspicion of any food that they wouldn't find back home. They also do not like their holiday enjoyment to be interrupted, especially during something as serious as bar room gambling, and extra especially not by someone who 'isn't our own'. Billies saw David, Joy and me as nothing but props in their holiday; they viewed us as 'having it easy with a life of sun, sand and sangria', when nothing could have been further from the truth. And so it's with great sadness that I hold up my hand and admit that by my sixth year in Tenerife, I too was guilty of regarding 'typical' holidaymakers with contempt and of having the word 'Billy' in my vocabulary.

~

That poor German man wasn't the only death in our lives during 1997, our sixth year in Tenerife. A loyal patron much closer to our hearts, who had seen us through thick and thin, protected us from unwanted advances and become an integral part of the Smugglers history also met his maker.

Ironically, it was one of the deceased's biggest enemies who blubbed the tragic news that Buster had been killed.

In the early days, Monsieur Claude from Chez Claude, the French restaurant on the level above us, had fought daily battles with our ginger protector. Feline stubbornness was pitched against Gallic aloofness and international relations were brought to straining point. As soon as Chez Claude opened, Buster decided that their cordon bleu fare was preferable to the everyday offerings in the Smugglers. Why settle for tuna straight from the can when you could have *salmon en papillote*? The only problem was Monsieur Claude wasn't willing to give it to him. And Buster wouldn't take no for an answer. Which is why the owner's youngest daughter had whistled at me from the upstairs railings on the day they had opened.

'*Tu*. Come,' she beckoned.

It was the first time I'd been in a 'proper' restaurant kitchen. Seven times as large as the Smugglers food engine, seventy times cleaner, and 700 times more organised. Gleaming stainless steel was everywhere – except for an angry patch of matted ginger on the white tiled floor. Buster stood there menacingly as Claude tried to fend him off with a stainless steel tureen lid and a long-handled soup ladle.

'He is yours, *non*?' raged Claude in his immaculate chef whites. 'We cannot have *un chat* in ze kitchen. Please, take eet away.'

'C'mon Buster,' I said, rubbing my thumb across two fingers to make that shushing sound that most cats seem taken by.

But Buster wasn't most cats. I was wary of picking him up, mindful of the damage he'd caused to unsuspecting bar customers who fancied themselves as cat-lovers. If he was not in a good mood, which he clearly wasn't, judging from the swish of his tail, he was also quite capable of literally biting the hand that fed him.

'One moment,' I said to Claude and hurried back downstairs, returning a moment later with a pair of black plastic maracas. Standing between Claude and Buster, I rattled the shakers as loud as I could. Buster eyeballed me for a second or two, then ambled away. We'd discovered that the only thing that Buster loathed more than dogs was Latin percussion. Actually, it was probably just maracas, but we never got to test him with castanets or timbales.

Armed with this knowledge – and since he had by now become immune to the water-pistol deterrent – we had reached a new understanding in our own kitchen downstairs. If he crossed the line from the terracotta tiles in the public area to the white ceramic tiles in the kitchen, we'd play him a percussive rhythm until he backed away. He soon learnt that there were boundaries in the Smugglers and he would sit at the very edge of danger, watching our every move and probably harbouring a deep mistrust of any Latin musician.

We encouraged Monsieur Claude to arm himself with a similar weapon, but he pooh-poohed the idea and was thus forced to hurl whatever stainless steel utensils were at hand to fend off the ginger intruder every day.

~

'*Ton chat, ton chat*,' sniffed Claude. 'Ee iz gone.'

Joy steadied herself on the mop handle. 'What do you mean, gone?'

'On ze street… at ze side… *un grand camion…* erm, lorry, no? Come, *toute suite*.' He beckoned Joy to follow, wiping tears as he strode out the door.

On the main road at the back of El Beril, a Dorada lorry had stopped in the middle of the road. The driver had his back to us. He held a red baseball cap by his side in one hand, and the other hand was clasped to the top of his head.

As we rushed nearer we could see a familiar ginger shape lying peacefully at the side of the road. But the angle of his body was anything but familiar, his grapefruit-sized head twisted almost 180 degrees. Buster's life had not ended peacefully. But it perhaps *had* ended in a manner befitting the arrogance and swagger of such a monumental cat, a cat who was prone to strutting across busy roads completely unperturbed by heavy-laden beer wagons such as this.

'What have you done, you stupid cat?' said Joy, crouching down and stroking him. She turned to the distraught lorry driver. 'We've only just given him a bath,' she cried, as if this knowledge would have made him brake that much harder.

Monsieur Claude slapped the lorry driver's arm with the back of his hand and tutted.

It was true that we'd only just bathed Buster. Apart from staring through the windscreen, paws on the dashboard as we took him on a car ride, Buster's second favourite treat was having a bath. He would quite happily leap straight into a bath full of water, regardless of the temperature. He would purr loudly as we massaged his oily fur with cat shampoo but would hiss if we dared wet his pudgy face. Despite the baths, he still sported a permanent single black stripe along the length of his back from prowling underneath vehicles in the El Beril car park. His frame was so large that his attempts to reach those elusive parts that needed licking clean always resulted in him rolling right over and giving up.

Two other cars had pulled over, aware that something tragic must have happened. Burt the timeshare wallah had also come striding across the road from his office in a bungalow at the top of El Beril. He looked gravely on. 'I'm a vet,' he said to Joy, gently placing a hand on her shoulder. 'Is there anything I can do?'

'We'd better get him off the road,' I said, and scooped Buster into my arms. He was still warm. I felt a compelling need to cuddle him but could feel bones grating in his neck, which made putting him back down more of an urgent issue.

We decided to bury him without ceremony, next to the road where he met his fate.

JOE CAWLEY

EVEN MORE KETCHUP THAN SALSA

Chapter Twenty

If Buster dying signalled the end of an era in our Tenerife lives, it was the dead body in the bar and subsequent lack of compassion from some of the customers that actually killed any remaining yearning to remain British bar owners abroad. The decision was taken that enough was enough. We decided to put the bar up for sale.

Although New Year's Eve had been a huge success and brought in sufficient funds to set us back on track, the fire had taken its toll physically and emotionally. Superhuman strength and the pulling together of our regulars had saved the night but part of our spirit had been lost in the smoke and debris. We really couldn't face another year of uphill struggle in a business that we no longer cared about.

If we hadn't owed so much money, I wouldn't have been bothered if the bar reopened or not. The feelings that had inspired us all to make it the best bar/restaurant in Tenerife were no longer there – namely pride, excitement, energy and interest. Instead, loathing, despair, exhaustion and boredom stood in our path, arms folded, like four burly bouncers intent on keeping us away from further success and happiness. We all knew our time had come. When David first broached the idea of selling the Smugglers, Joy and I readily agreed.

The original plan had been to give it five years then return with our new-found riches to join the ranks of successful entrepreneurs back in Blighty. Six years had now passed; most of that time had

211

been enjoyable, some of it had been painful, and a great deal of it had been bewildering.

We'd taken the Smugglers Tavern as far as we could in an ever-changing climate. It was spring 1997 and Tenerife was no longer the sole preserve of sun-starved Brits. Other nationalities had discovered the island's pleasures, and more to the point, the pleasures of the Altamira and El Beril, while a proportion of our yearly regulars had found new playgrounds in the cheap, rising stars of tourism like Bulgaria and Turkey. UK tour operators had had a record year, flinging nearly 16 million people to various parts of the world, and package-holiday-destination options had multiplied eightfold, but Tenerife was no longer the first name out of the hat.

David's job of writing all the daily blackboards had also increased eightfold: he now had to do the menus in English, French, German, Spanish, Italian, Hungarian, Norwegian, Swedish and Russian. We had to tailor our entertainment programme accordingly, staging only events that had international appeal, which ruled out the ever-popular quiz nights and Bingo brawls.

We decided to keep the news quiet, telling only a few of our closest allies such as Wayne, Robin, Sammy and Barry until we'd formally put the bar and business up for sale with an agent. Inevitably, by the very next morning everybody knew.

Some were shocked, some were sympathetic and a few told us that they knew our hearts hadn't been in it for a while now. 'Might buy it myself,' was the second most common phrase we'd hear, but 'How much are you selling it for?' was the clear winner.

EVEN MORE KETCHUP THAN SALSA

Despite all the attention, real enquiries were non-existent. It would take almost twelve more months of begrudging toil before we finally got some genuine interest.

~

As 1997 turned into 1998, we pondered lowering the price and accepting a small loss on the sale, so desperate were we to escape. Regular clients had begun to notice signs of despair and increasing frustration – such as Joy bursting into tears whenever anybody in the know asked if we'd sold it yet. But, as often happens, fate intervened when we were at rock bottom and the tide turned.

As well as becoming a popular micro destination for holidaymakers, sunshine property owners and timeshare purchasers, our little patch of southwest Tenerife had turned into a magnet for mini-mafias – Sicily with sangria, if you like. Gangs had their own zones of operation, depending on where they stood in the hierarchy. The black trenchcoats and leather jackets of Micky and his crew – the father-and-son mobsters who'd called the Smugglers their local when they lived in El Beril in our first six months – were still regularly seen skulking around a villa HQ closer to the centre of La Caleta village. JP's lot were more notorious, more sophisticated and a little more clandestine, apparently using methods of money extraction that didn't just entail turning up in big boots and demanding it; the smoked windscreens of their supposedly anonymous 4x4s dominated the driveways of several luxurious villas nearby. Novice gangsters in the early days of their chosen careers also hung around El Beril, learning the ropes in a much more open fashion.

Surprisingly, the Italians were some of the last to join Tenerife's gangland party. Don Carlos and his entourage had arrived on the El Beril scene six months earlier. Overnight he took over the hairdressing salon next to the Altamira reception, turned the empty *local* between ourselves and Patricia's supermarket into a competing supermarket, and opened a fashion boutique on the floor above us, next but one to Bar Arancha.

The Smugglers was being observed, that much was obvious. Don Carlos, his wife and his newly arrived son Fabio would regularly sit at a table in our bar, following our every move with silent and disconcerting attention. Neither Joy, David or I had ever actually heard them speak, their preferred method of communication being a series of points and grunts. It was only when Fabio was sent to open up a dialogue that we realised why he in particular was of the quiet, mysterious persuasion.

'Hello?' said a voice several octaves above what you could call manly.

Joy and I were crouched behind the bar at the time, replacing the worn stack of beer mats that were propping up one corner of the beer fridge. We looked at each other, unsure as to whether the rotund figure peering over the bar top with the receding hairline and brown slacks buckled high over his navel was attempting to make us laugh. His deadpan expression suggested otherwise.

'My father, he want talk with you.' Fabio held my gaze. 'Now.'

Joy and I let go of the beer fridge, loosening a cascade of Dorada bottles that rattled and rolled in its metal innards, and went to sit with Don Carlos and his wife, who, it transpired, spoke no English whatsoever. Don Carlos spoke to us through his son.

'He says how much for the place?' squeaked Fabio.

'Erm... fifty-five million pesetas for the business and *local*,' said Joy. 'Freehold.' We were both a little taken back by the suddenness of the approach. 'I can show you the books if you like. It's a very good—'

Fabio was already consulting with his father and interrupted. 'No need. He'll give you fifty million.'

Joy and I looked at each other again. Was he serious? Had we just sold the bar? Was it that easy? 'Right, well, erm... that's very good... I mean, great. Shall we shake on it?'

Don Carlos whispered into Fabio's ear.

'Come to our office upstairs at five and he will give you cheque for five million pesetas deposit.'

All three of them rose from the table and left without a handshake or anything.

Joy and I rushed into the kitchen as fast as we could without breaking into a trot. We both punched the air in victory.

'Do you think they're serious?' said Joy.

'Sounds like it, but we'll know for sure if they give us a cheque tonight.'

'So long as it doesn't bounce,' she added, her cynicism a constant companion these days.

That evening the deposit was presented with as big a fanfare as the announcement that Don Carlos wanted to buy the Smugglers – in other words, none. He quickly scrawled his signature, then handed us a cheque for five million pesetas as though he were paying for a delivery of bananas.

Jack, our stepfather, had faxed over a contract of sale template that he had used many times before. In a raft of addenda, appendices, clauses and sub-clauses it outlined that fact that basically Don Carlos had agreed to take the Smugglers off our hands – lock, stock and urinals – for a pre-determined fee that had to be paid within ninety days. The contract was deemed valid after a non-returnable deposit of 10 per cent had been paid (without bouncing). Which it didn't. So we had sold. Which was nice.

Actually, it was like winning the lottery and being released from a long stretch in prison on the same day. Forehead creases disappeared; shoulders dropped into relaxed mode for the first time in years; and Tenerife suddenly took on the role of paradise island rather than foreign jailer.

The sky turned several shades bluer and the palm trees lining the El Beril road were no longer sentries guarding the entrance but exotic reminders of a sub-tropical existence. It was as though literally at the flick of a switch – or the handing over of a cheque in this case – our world of black and white had been flooded with a palette of Technicolor hues.

For the next three months no customer could shatter the dreamlike state David, Joy and I were floating in, no matter how hard they tried, which inevitably they did. Even Friedhelm seemed bearable.

216

EVEN MORE KETCHUP THAN SALSA

After the euphoria of release came the excitement of planning ahead. For the first time in my life, armed with a wad of cash, the options seemed endless. Australia, America and Tahiti all crossed my mind. So did Bolton, but understandably not with quite as much gusto as the former trio.

While Joy and I prodded, poked and fondled various ideas about what to do with the rest of our lives, David and Andi set the wheels in motion for a return to the UK punctuated by wedding bells. It was the happiest I had ever seen my brother. A new life with a new partner complete with new-found riches and an open road ahead. How much better could it get?

Much of their time was spent planning the ceremony, with Andi making frequent weekend trips back to the UK to choose the venue and caterers, pick a dress and send out wedding invitations. It was to be a late-July wedding, allowing two months after our final days at the Smugglers to move back to England, assuming Don Carlos took the full ninety days before handing over the balance.

We pored over the brochure of the country house they had booked in Mold, Cheshire. The aerial shot on the cover showed a honey-stoned stately home framed with ivy and encircled by fields freckled with yellow and white blooms. Rich green oaks and sycamore trees surrounded the mansion and tossed lazy shadows across shaved lawns. It was England. And it beckoned us all.

~

Running the bar with an end date in mind altered everything. On the one hand the discipline was gone. Opening and closing times were regulated more by whim than rule. While this infuriated some of our customers, it felt like we were in control again rather than being governed by what the patrons demanded. Several of them were unhappy with our 'choice' of new owners. They wanted the Smugglers to remain a bastion of little Britain in El Beril, their local in a foreign land. They realised that Italian ownership would mean a change of focus, ambience and food.

On a practical level we also had to start thinking about reducing stock. We didn't want to be left with dozens of bottles of spirits and portions of frozen meat and we certainly didn't want to end up giving it away to the new Italian owners. Reciting what wasn't on the menu or available behind the bar became one of Joy's daily rituals, but the huffs and puffs of disgruntled diners went sailing over her head.

If breaking the chains provided inordinate relief from everyday demands, something that did silently gnaw at the euphoria was the behaviour of Don Carlos and the growing number of Italians who'd arrived to join Fabio's high-waistband gang over the past few weeks. It was a niggle that we dared not voice though.

Before the sale, the family had been frequent if somewhat unsociable patrons. Now they became conspicuous by their absence. We assumed that having purchased yet another business in El Beril they would be busy plotting, planning and measuring up for the changes that they intended to make at the Smugglers. But there was none of that.

We also thought that, as we were now playing an integral role in their expanding empire, they would become a little friendlier towards us. But on the rare occasions that we passed Fabio in the car park, smiles were as scarce as ever. Still, as Joy reminded me, we hadn't sold the bar to make friends, we'd sold it to make money, retain our sanity and move on to something new.

May 20th was the date by which full payment had to be made, but it came and went without any mention, or sign of further money. After seven years of running the bar, a few more weeks wouldn't make much difference, I reassured myself, although the freezer and bottle shelves were beginning to look a little bleak by now.

By May 25th the gnawing worry had turned into overwhelming anxiety. 'Everything okay, Fabio?' I asked as he we passed in the Altamira reception.

'Yes, yes,' he squealed.

'Good. Good. Nice day today, yes?'

'Yes. Nice.'

'Business going okay?'

'Oh for God's sake,' Joy muttered, pushing in front of me. 'Fabio, what's going on with your dad? He needs to pay us the rest of the money for the bar. Will you tell him?'

'Sure,' said Fabio, and walked off.

Later that day Joy and I were stocktaking what little stock we had left in the kitchen when David walked in.

'Just seen Squeaky,' he said. 'His dad wants to see us in his office.'

'At last!' said Joy.

219

'We should get Sammy and Robin in tonight and go and celebrate,' said David.

We all agreed, then David and I strolled across to the Altamira office of Don Carlos.

'We'll need to give him a receipt of some sort, I should imagine,' I said to David.

'He'll probably have it all set out himself,' he replied. 'We'll just need to sign for it.'

I nodded. 'Gonna be weird actually giving him the keys, isn't it?'

'Not before time,' he smiled. 'After you...' He pushed open the glass door.

Don Carlos glanced up from behind a white desk and gave the barest of nods. Fabio stood beside him and gestured to two seats.

This was the moment. This was when the seven years of blood, sweat and woe finally came to an end. This was when the heartbreak of ruined relationships, the pounding stress and manic pretence of being everybody's best friend stopped. This was the time when it all suddenly seemed worth it – well, most of it.

'My father doesn't want the bar now,' said Fabio abruptly.

All peripheral vision disappeared as I tried to focus on the words, the deadpan expression, waiting for a punchline. A sickness reared, the same feeling I had had in the kitchen when I'd found Joy with Steve. My heart tightened and heat rose within my chest, filling my head with an intensity that showed no signs of abating.

The silence seemed to last minutes. I tried to swallow but couldn't.

'What do you mean?' said a quiet voice by my

side.

'Our…' Fabio paused, '… situation has changed. We don't wish to buy the bar now.' Our shock must have been clearly visible. 'Sorry,' he added.

I managed to find my voice. 'But you paid a deposit. Five million.'

'We know.'

'The contract says that you lose it if you don't complete the purchase,' said David.

Fabio shrugged. 'We know. My father says keep it. We agreed.' He moved to the door and ushered us out. 'Sorry,' he added again.

David and I stood outside, the door closed on our dreams. Shit,' he said, fumbling in his shirt pocket for a cigarette. 'That's the wedding out the window.'

'Joy's gonna go spare,' I said.

~

Joy was humming to herself, polishing the mirrors behind the bottle shelves. She turned round, having seen us arrive in the reflection.

'Show me the money,' she grinned, her hands raised, holding Glassex and dustcloth. They dropped quickly to her side as she took in our blank expressions. 'What? What's up?'

'He's backed out,' I said quietly.

'Sorry?'

'The Italians, they don't want to buy it anymore.'

'But… but… they've paid a deposit. We signed a contract. What do you mean?' Her eyes welled up. 'We agreed. They said they wanted it. They can't pull out.'

221

David lit another cigarette. 'I'd better go tell Andi.'

Joy slumped into a chair, ashen-faced. 'I can't carry on, Joe, I can't.'

'I know,' I said. 'Neither can I.'

Chapter Twenty-One

A grey mist of gloom hung over the bar for the following fortnight as we resentfully built the stock back up again. Getting up at eight every morning after a 2am bedtime became even more of a battle. We were completely defenceless in the face of our new despondency: our last remaining weapons – hope and liberation – had been unceremoniously ripped from our hands. David and Andi were resigned to the fact that the wedding was now not going to happen and were negotiating with the owners of the country house in Mold to get their deposit back. We were all trapped in huge debt in a business that faced increasing competition and dwindling custom.

Tel had long since abandoned the price parity agreement, dropping the cost of his drinks to lure those who were more cash-conscious than loyal. We thought about following suit but decided against it, keeping the price of a pint at 250 pesetas as opposed to his 200. However, whereas before customers were compensated with a cheery welcome and friendly banter in the Smugglers – two qualities that were noticeably lacking at Tel's – nowadays these assets were missing from our bar too.

We weren't the only bar to be struggling in the south of Tenerife though. Out of every charter flight of 250 sunburned holidaymakers departing Reina Sofia Airport it seemed that at least half were set to return weeks later to open up a new Pheasant Plucker, Lancashire Pride or Dirty Dick's Bar. The

223

damn things were popping up faster than bubbles in a shandy, each one offering karaoke, chicken and chips for 350 pesetas and pints of beer cheaper than their neighbours. Which was great for customers looking for value for their pound but meant that the new landlord would inevitably be heading for a sticky wicket, having overlooked the wise words of Dickens in *David Copperfield*: 'Annual income twenty pounds, annual expenditure nineteen [pounds] nineteen [shillings] and six [pence], result happiness. Annual income twenty pounds, annual expenditure twenty pounds ought and six, result misery.'

While those on one side of the bar made the most of the cheap revelry, those on the other side drowned in financial misery. Freshly painted signs announcing 'Gary and Maureen from Barnsley Welcome You to The Pits' would barely have time to dry in the tropical breeze before the shutters would come down; the signs themselves would then be packed away in suitcases along with what little was left of the owners' lives and flown back to Leeds Bradford Airport with Gary and Maureen undoubtedly on separate flights.

Six months seemed to be the standard career length for enthusiastic new bar owners. Most trod a familiar path:

Month 1: Wave goodbye to Blighty
Month 2: Wave goodbye to all your life savings
Months 3 & 4: Develop a typical capital 'D' expat shape and a formidable dependence on alcohol
Month 5: Wave goodbye to your long-suffering spouse with the words 'I should never have listened to you' still ringing in your ears
Month 6: Wave goodbye to Tenerife, wearing all

you now own (faded T-shirt and swim shorts, stolen hotel slippers and fake Rolex haggled from a 'lucky-lucky' man)

We knew we were the exceptions, having done remarkably well to have lasted seven years, but there was no way we could carry on much longer. We needed a miracle.

We got Father Christmas – or at least someone bearing an uncanny resemblance.

~

If it wasn't for the fact that Bernie was from Walsall, owned a building company and drank brandy from a pint glass, you wouldn't have been able to resist sitting on his knee, telling him what a good boy or girl you'd been and asking after the wellbeing of his elves.

With his long white hair, silvery beard, deep-throated chortle and weight-induced waddle he was every inch a festive lookalike. And he'd brought us a present.

Bernie owned several villas in El Beril, most of which were regularly occupied by one or more of his inordinate number of offspring. Anybody who asked for a beer in a Midlands accent seemed to be genetically linked to Bernie, but the man himself was an infrequent visitor, only usually venturing in at Christmas and New Year.

'Still here then?' he said, rather obviously, sipping on a pint of 103 brandy. He was perched uneasily on a bar stool, half on half off, as though he couldn't decide whether to sit or stand. 'What happened to them Spanish that were supposed to be buying you out?'

'Italians,' corrected Joy.

'Same thing,' said Bernie.

'They pulled out,' I said. 'A change in circumstances, apparently.'

'We got to keep the five million deposit though,' smiled Joy weakly.

'So you're going to carry on for a few more years?'

'I hope not,' said Joy quickly. 'We're desperate to get out.'

Bernie slurped out the last of his brandy. He sucked in his breath through clenched teeth. 'Could take you ages to find another buyer,' he said, shaking his head. 'How much were you asking?'

'Fifty-five million originally. But we dropped to fifty.'

Bernie paused. 'Tell you what, you've already had five million. I'll give you the other forty-five and we're both happy.'

I smiled and sighed inwardly, having heard so many false offers and bullshit from customers 'thinking' about buying the Smugglers from us. But Bernie wasn't smiling back. His gaze flicked from Joy to me.

I stopped smiling. 'You're serious? *You* want to buy the bar? Why?'

'It's a good business. You've let it go recently, but new owners, fresh faces… that's all it needs.'

'Oh, thanks,' said Joy sarcastically.

'And a damn good clean.' Bernie lifted his pint glass and turned the lipstick mark towards us. There was no denying we had lost all pride in the bar. It was plain to see it needed a lot of TLC. 'Anyway, you know where I am,' said Bernie heaving his bulk off the stool. 'You won't get a better offer the state it's in now. Take what you can and run. That's my advice. Go see the world. You're too young to be stuck for the rest of your lives in this dump. See ya.'

Joy and I looked at each other. A big beam broke out on her face. 'Did we just sell the bar again?'

~

It all seemed slightly too good to be true, and in a way it was. Not only was Bernie getting a steal, but one of the conditions of sale was that we took part cash plus one of his properties, a new-build villa on Golf Las Américas.

This oasis of greenery decorating the rocky dumping ground that separated Las Américas from Los Cristianos had been the talk of Tenerife when plans were first announced in a glare of self-congratulatory press releases in the local paper, *Island Connections*. It would be a life-giving injection of diversity on an island that had become dependent on selling just sun, sand and sea. With the advent of so many similar, and cheaper, package holiday destinations, the powers that be realised that the island now needed to attract wealthier holidaymakers as well.

Unsurprisingly the topic had been batted back and forth among residents with too much time on their hands. Some were adamant that this patch of grass was to become a championship golf course owned and run by Seve Ballesteros, while others were certain that it marked the start of Disneyland being built in Las Américas. This drew on one of Tenerife's longest-running urban myths, though how golf and Mickey Mouse had become associated on an island in much greater need of more reality than more fantasy escaped logic.

The offer from Bernie wasn't ideal, especially as we all wanted to tidy up every last loose end in Tenerife before returning to the UK, but as David sensibly reminded us, the property came with a guaranteed rental income on an in-demand golf complex and thus would provide a small but steady income to fill the gap between leaving the bar and starting a new business or job in England. Plus the property should be a doddle to sell.

Bernie had us over the proverbial barrel. He knew we were desperate, was fully aware that not many wannabe bar owners could afford to buy the building as well as the business and wasn't afraid to let us know that he considered he was doing us a favour. But before we had time to get him to sign a 'Bought as Seen' contract, the Conditions of Sale list began to grow longer by the day.

After making us accept one of his properties in part-payment, he next insisted we pay for the outside terrace tiles to be replaced. Following closer inspection of the kitchen, he also demanded a new fridge, one without an infestation of cockroaches, which we couldn't deny was reasonable. Then he wanted new upholstery, a complete fumigation, air conditioning installed and for at least two of us to stay on for a minimum of one month to train one of his untrainable offspring in how to manage a bar.

We agreed to the fumigation, fridge and new tiles outside but drew the line at the rest and thankfully he backed down without argument. It seemed we had reached a final deal but we still felt as though we were walking on eggshells until the day arrived to go to the notary and make it all official.

The morning felt like it should have ceremony. It was to be a momentous occasion and deserved a little pomp. I wanted to savour the day, conscious of each trivial task and the part it played in the parade. I brushed my teeth staring in the mirror reminding myself that this was the last time I'd brush my teeth as owner of the Smugglers Tavern. With cupped hands and tepid water I damped down the flames of hair protruding from one side of my head and noted that this would also probably be the last day in my life when I could say I owned a urinal. My usual snatched bowl of Cocoa Puffs became a commemorative meal, a memory to be gathered and held special, one of those big moments locked in my mind, like the day we first assembled in the Smugglers kitchen, delirious from a cocktail of excitement and fear as Mario introduced us to the shiny new utensils of our chosen trade.

Or like the day I left Glossop Comprehensive, emerging after that last bell into a glorious Derbyshire Friday knowing that the coming weekend would be different. It wouldn't be just a revolving platform returning me to the same place again and again but a path to a world that had suddenly opened up beyond the confines of nine till four; no more facing the regiments of identical desks and chairs or watching the mouths of teachers opening and closing in a faraway hum as they droned facts and figures that were of little interest to hormone-heavy teenagers.

That Friday we tramped into the rolling hills of the Peak District, running our hands over furry patches of moss on dry limestone walls and bleating back at complaining sheep, marching just far enough into the countryside to a grassy fold where Old Glossop could be seen no more, and more importantly where we became invisible to the world. Here we sat chatting, scrawling witty messages on each other's white school shirts and passing round a bottle of fruity Bulmers cider for the very last time.

It was freedom, liberty, the unshackling of chains, the lifting of restrictions – whatever you want to call it, *that* was the common denominator in nearly all of my special moments. Situations that involved the imposing of new boundaries or limitations, such as the beginning of a new school term or the starting of a new job, were never celebrated with the same passion and gusto. It's true that beginnings also held a certain excitement – the thrill of the unknown, a change in routine and an eye-opening stimulation of all the senses – but they weren't the same. Even childhood Christmases, exhilarating as they were, didn't bring the explosive elation that came with something ending.

The ending of something is the ultimate high; like death, I suppose. Perhaps that in part explains the appeal of suicide, for people like my dad. Do they finally figure that the euphoric freedom from their demons lies in two little words – 'The End' – so long as it really is the end, and doesn't entail yet another new beginning, with all its ensuing inherent worries and effort?

For those of us who seek inner calm and mindful contentment, nothing beats an ending. The problem is that although this feeling is so liberating and so fulfilling, it only lasts until the next beginning. My yearning for that sensation was almost an addiction and the only way to feed the habit was to bring about more and more endings, which inevitably resulted in more and more beginnings and a succession of intense but short-term life commitments.

'Your sleeve's in your Cocoa Puffs,' interrupted Joy. It was time to go to the notary and sign away the Smugglers.

~

Notaries hold great sway in Spain, trusted without demur and held in high esteem by those who know that nothing of great importance gets passed without the approval of this God-like figure. As David, Andi, Joy and I waited in the crowded reception area for Bernie and his solicitor to show up, it felt as if we were grooms at the altar awaiting our brides. Our appointment was at 10.15 on June 5th 1998, almost seven years to the day since we'd started the whole silly caper. The white clock above the reception desk showed it was 10.14. Bernie was leaving it late. My stomach started to churn, mouth dry.

Ten twenty came and went and still no Bernie. I was now feeling decidedly nauseous. Could it happen again? Could this be another failed sale? After two more anxiety-filled minutes spent watching the clock, a slim, middle-aged lady with her hair in the most elevated bun I had ever seen approached and asked if we were ready to go in. Our solicitor explained that the purchaser still hadn't shown up. The lady pushed back her white cotton sleeve and glanced at her dainty watch. We were reminded that the notary was a very important man and could only wait another few minutes before we'd have to schedule another appointment.

We knew that if Bernie didn't show in the next few minutes we most certainly wouldn't be needing another appointment, thank you very much. We'd all need a straitjacket and a ride to the nearest home for the mentally exhausted. Joy looked at me, I looked at Andi, Andi looked at David, David smoked from the side of his mouth.

A few moments later Bernie arrived, out of breath and clutching a folder bulging with papers. We were ushered quickly into the notary's office. Gold-framed certificates dotted the wood panelling, each one reinforcing the importance of the serious-looking man who was sitting stony-faced at the distant edge of an enormous expanse of cedar, a surface large and sturdy enough for a bout of tag-team wrestling.

He peered over his glasses as we shuffled in and then gestured to the vacant chairs with the tip of a silver pen. A secretary scurried in, thrust a document under his nose and whispered in his ear. She smiled. He didn't. But he did make a show of signing each page of the document as it was flipped open for him. Each signature involved a one-armed dance, a miniature flamenco comprising a flourish of inky curves followed by a vigorous final dot that looked and sounded like it would leave an indent on the polished wood.

As the document was whisked away, he sat back, gazing along the line of us like a headmaster about to reprimand a class.

'*Vamos*,' he smiled. Let's go.

The next ten minutes involved a succession of pen-swapping, and the occasional glance up at our solicitor for sage nods of approval, as we signed an interminable ream of paperwork passed our way by the secretary, who relayed the documents back and forth, breaking into a little jog each time she hurried back to His Royal Highness until finally… it was over.

David, Andi, Joy and I drove back to the bar, the atmosphere in the car strangely subdued. I'd expected euphoria on confirmation of the unshackling, but instead felt like I was breaking up with a girlfriend. In El Beril, the four of us gazed down at the Smugglers from the upper-level railings. The bar *looked* the same, but something about it had definitely changed. It no longer felt like ours, no longer seemed like our second home. Just like when Joy and I broke up, I felt detached. The Smugglers was the Smugglers, and I was Joe again, not Smugglers' Joe. The bar stood like an empty theatre, waiting for the next troupe of actors to bring it to life with a new era of love, laughter and tears, both behind the scenes and front of house.

For somebody else now, this bar on the outskirts of La Caleta would dictate their life. Undoubtedly it would provide highs: ringing with merriment on party nights when the right combination of easy-going holidaymakers consuming moderate levels of alcohol bounced off the banter of fresh-faced proprietors who had yet to become weary from continual late nights and Groundhog Days of subservience – shop, prep, cook, clean… shop, prep, cook, clean…

There would of course also be the lows of relationships strained to breaking point by the demands of this high-maintenance mistress; nights of sleeplessness when the hum of the beer coolers would be louder than the ring of the till; and the hair-pulling frustration of attending to day-to-day bureaucracy that ate up the day while the bar remained closed.

Bernie had returned and joined us at the railings.

'She's all yours now,' I said. 'I guess you'll be wanting these.' I dropped the keys into his outstretched hand.

This was really it. We were done. David and Andi set off down the hill to their apartment. I put an arm round Joy and we strolled the opposite way.

~

I woke early, earlier than I had had to every other morning for the past seven years. The sun illuminated a shaft of dust though a parting in our bedroom curtains, its particles twirling and spinning like a child's merry-go-round. I watched it for a moment as thoughts tumbled into place. Autopilot had already kicked in, nagging me to get up and prepare to open the bar. But like a film on extreme fast-forward, dozens of images spun through my mind. As I pushed back the sheets I felt the cold of Bolton market and saw Darren trudging around with a rabbit's head in the hood of his snorkel jacket, Seafood Sandra trying to round up her fleeing crabs and the sincere, almost pleading look in the eyes of Pat, the stall owner, when he asked if we had any jobs going in Tenerife. Where would we be now, if we'd never escaped from the market?

The living room was still dark as my hand felt along the wall for the light switch. One memory triggered another as I recalled having to wedge the bar's electricity trip-switch to 'on' with a plank of wood, electrocuting myself with a cable stretched from one of the apartments, nearly poisoning our punters with a cockroach fumigation. Thousands of people (and creatures) had come through our doors over the past seven years, bringing thousands of dramas – Wayne and Frank and their crazy DIY disasters, Micky the hoodlum, Buster the irascible ginger bar cat, and of course Steve, relationship-wrecker.

I opened the curtains slightly to see the sun slowly spreading a golden haze over the Adeje mountains and I smiled as my mind focused on a close-up of the Smugglers keys being dropped into Bernie's hand. I could still hear the jingling as the key to the double front doors rattled with all the other keys to the little kingdom that was no longer ours: the store room on the opposite side of the terrace, the beer barrels that were chained together outside, the propane gas cupboard next to the window. And the till key, the tiniest of all, but the keeper of what this seven-year rollercoaster ride had been all about.

I sat down on one of the white plastic patio chairs and felt the warmth of the early sun. The aroma of strong coffee rose from the mug cupped close to my chest like a familiar friend. Life felt good. I revelled in the moment, the euphoria of success celebrated in perfect surroundings.

Beyond the bay of El Duque, at the far end of the arcing curve, Playa de Las Américas and Los Cristianos would be coming to life, shop owners, timeshare salespeople, bar workers and entertainers ready to face a new day's challenge in 'Paradise'. I remembered the assortment of entertainers we'd hired, like our 4 foot 10, helium-voiced Elvis who took just two songs to empty the bar, and the pompous Gastón with his Mystique magic show that ended with the stage collapsing and his assistant freewheeling into the wall while trapped inside a sawn-in-half prop box. Good times.

While we had the bar, the barrage of challenges we faced on a daily basis made it difficult to focus on the enjoyable side of the job. But now, wallowing in the luxury of unpressured hindsight, I could see that we had indeed enjoyed *many* good times and we'd met many good people, made friends that returned and kept in touch with letters and postcards. The business had provided us with a good income for most of the time, and now had enabled us to step off its crazy merry-go-round with a sizeable profit and an enormous sense of satisfaction.

From the terrace the Atlantic appeared still, untroubled by the waves and currents that a new day would inevitably bring. On the horizon, the island of La Gomera had started to emerge from the haze and beyond that… well, anything could lie beyond the horizon. England was calling, but having made the move once, broken free of the geographical restrictions that most people self-impose, anywhere in the world now seemed possible. For me this was a perfect ending, unsullied by the worrisome burden of having to start something new. At least for that one glorious morning in Tenerife.

Epilogue

Needless to say, it was a big shock going from working fourteen-hour days, seven days a week for a full seven years to waking up to days of, well, nothing. For the first few weeks there was a gaping hole. I felt like I *should* be doing something, a niggle in the back of my mind that things were being left unattended to, like the feeling you have when you think you've left the house without turning the frying pan off. It was disconcerting and both Joy and I set about cleaning the apartment, moving furniture around and generally keeping busy because we thought we had to. It took several weeks before we realised we didn't.

In the meantime, Bernie had started renovating the Smugglers. I didn't dare venture in for fear of reviving those old feelings of stress. In fact, both Joy and I tried our best to avoid going even within sight of the bar. But occasionally while walking to the car I'd spy out of the corner of my eye our old padded cushions dumped on the terrace along with pots of paint, brushes and dust sheets.

Instead of putting his son in charge, Bernie decided to rent out the bar. Very quickly it was taken over by an Argentinean family, who renamed it Lorenzo's, a name that continues to this day, emblazoned on the bright yellow canopy in the El Beril complex. Initially the Argentineans promoted it more as a restaurant than as a drinking venue, but they soon realised that there was a bigger profit to be made as a holiday 'bar'. Apparently, their Russian karaoke nights were by far the most popular, which, for David, Andi, Joy and me, confirmed that we had definitely got out at the right time.

Shortly after we sold the Smugglers, David and Andi moved back to the UK. We attended their perfect English wedding in the country house, along with a number of patrons who had remained friends, including Siobhan and Mike from Northern Ireland and Barry our obstinate quiz master. With the proceeds from the bar, David and Andi bought England's oldest post office, in the chocolate-box village of Chipping, but soon realised that they had plopped out of the pan and into the fryer. Living in a small village and providing a service to local residents and plentiful day-trippers proved too similar to the goldfish-bowl world of El Beril. They sold after a few years and now live in Clitheroe, close to the nursing home where our nan resides. Shortly before this book was completed, we all attended Nan's 105th birthday party in the home. She remains mentally bright and alert, even though her ailing body has ruled out a return to a catering career.

As for Joy and me, after almost twelve months of complete freedom, punctuated with the odd bout of casual labour in the form of apartment maintenance, we decided to leave Tenerife for good. Having sold the golf course villa that we'd received as part-payment for the Smugglers Tavern, we packed up most of our belongings and started to ship everything back to the UK.

Although by now we were revelling in the freedom and had plenty of cash in the bank, we felt like we'd lost our sense of belonging in Tenerife. Without the Smugglers Tavern operating as a

British bar and serving as a centre of focus for El Beril, the community spirit in the complex seemed to dissolve, and with it our connection to the place. Tel's Bar became the new meeting point for expat residents and UK holidaymakers, but due to our previous altercations as competitors Joy and I weren't inclined to frequent it. This compounded our feeling of being left out.

On the odd occasions when past customers returned and invited us out for a meal, I noticed that Joy's subconscious obligation to 'perform' as hostess resurfaced like a bad spirit that couldn't be contained. It scared me. Her own feisty, fun-loving personality had only just regained power and it was painful to see how easy it was for her to slip back into bar mode again. All of this hastened our decision to return to Blighty.

Obviously our main concern was what the heck we were going to do back there. The possibility of taking over a pub or restaurant in the UK was raised: 'Well, you've plenty of experience now. You know you can do it.' The idea was instantly dropped, and with a resounding thud punctuated with an emphatic 'Never. Again.'

The one idea that did stick was to run a bed and breakfast in a UK holiday resort. We'd be able to work from home, become part of a community again and put to good use all the experience that we'd gained. It seemed to tick all the right boxes and we set about seeking the perfect property on a one-week scouting mission back to Blighty.

It was while driving through the deserted streets of Llandudno in April, with windscreen wipers swishing furiously across our field of vision, that the decision was made. We'd seen three businesses for sale. All were struggling and all were staffed by couples who exhibited behaviour that was only too familiar.

When we were being shown round, they were initially exuberant, enthusiastic about the business, but half an hour later, as Joy grilled them to within an inch of their sanity, we saw the frailties surfacing: the resentment at having to pander to guests' every last wish at all times of the day and night, the battles with bureaucracy, particularly with the ever-changing health and hygiene regulations, and ultimately the wedge that had been driven through their relationship as a result of working and living together in such a demanding environment. The simmering ill-will and subtle snipes at each other's failings became clearer with every comment:

'Of course, Derek tries to stay out of their way as much as possible, don't you, Derek? You leave all the dirty work to me, don't you, Derek?'

'What we make in profit, *she* spends on redecorating every other week!'

'We live in the basement studio so we can rent out all the other rooms. Her Highness, here, isn't very happy, but it's the only way we make it pay.'

Joy and I came to the same face-slapping realisation at the same time. What in God's name were we doing? We'd be trapping ourselves in the same high-pressure, all-consuming, relationship-snapping environment as the Smugglers all over again!

Within weeks we'd shipped all of our personal belongings back to Tenerife, hoisted up the drawbridge and were cowering in the corner pondering our near escape. Why would we want to run a bed and breakfast joint in a British summer resort that rarely actually gets a summer? Why indeed would we want to move back to the UK? For what? All we needed to do was stay in Tenerife but live somewhere other than within a holiday complex. A quiet retreat in the hills was beckoning. Maybe get a gentle, unchallenging job. We could grow peppers, vines and make our own wine. Enjoy our little cocoon in rural Tenerife, appreciating each other and the simple things in life. But apparently that was not what fate had in store for me.

Little did I know that within twelve months I'd be swimming in shark-infested waters in the middle of the Nicaraguan jungle, tracking bears in the forests of Transylvania and ice-fishing in the Arctic Circle. But in the words of one of my favourite childhood TV programmes, that's another story.

~ THE END

If you enjoyed *Even More Ketchup than Salsa*, it would be mighty useful if you could *please, please, please* leave a review on Amazon by typing the following link into your web browser. Success for indie authors is all about word of mouth.
(Did I say '*please?*')

http://getbook.at/EvenMoreK

Acknowledgements

As with all creations that appear out of the ether, although the initial thoughts, creativity and process of spilling words onto a screen come down to the author, it just wouldn't have been possible without the help and support of many others.

Firstly I'd like to thank Joy, for agreeing to let me air our dirty laundry, so to speak. Those of you who have read both books about our Smugglers days will by now know enough about her to realise that if she had said 'You're not putting that!', it most certainly would not have appeared in the book. Understandably, she was at first reticent to share such intimate details of our relationship, but thankfully she agreed that I could tell our story, for the good of the story and to clearly demonstrate the huge pressure involved in working together in such a time-, energy- and personality-sapping environment. But that's not where my thanks stop when it comes to Joy. I also need to thank her for her patience, encouragement and unwavering support throughout my writing career thus far.

You'll have met my mum too if you read the first book, *More Ketchup than Salsa.* Mum, or Carole to you, has backed me through each and every one of my dreams – first as a musician, then as a computer programmer (don't ask), and now as a writer. As well as a great deal of encouragement and support, she has also exhibited an inordinate amount of love and pride, both throughout our Smugglers days and now.

I'd like to thank my stepdad Jack as well, for offering us the opportunity to turn our lives around when all we were doing was ambling down a pleasant yet meaningless path. When the financial situation at Smugglers took a dip, Jack was very lenient and generous over the terms of our loan when by all rights he could have exerted more pressure.

I'm sure my brother David feels the same way, and he is another person that I'd like to thank, principally for not slapping me about the head for some of the things I wrote about him. Sorry, bruv!

There's another character in the book whom I'd like to publicly acknowledge. My nan, who is aged 105 as this book goes to print, never ceases to amaze me with her resilience, canniness and courage. I may have concentrated on her less lucid moments in the writing of this book for comedic effect, but far from being batty, she is still incredibly with it and her fortitude in overcoming personal tragedies has, and always will be, an inspiration.

Second lastly, but not second leastly, I'd like to thank my editor, Lucy Ridout. Lucy has been the epitome of professionalism when pointing out the error of my wordy ways, when I'm sure she would have much rather screamed 'How did you ever get through school!' or something like that. And yes, Lucy, I know 'leastly' is not an actual word.

Finally, thanks to you not only for buying my book(s) but for allocating part of your precious lifespan to reading my words. We all only have a certain number of hours in our day/week/month/year/life and I often think how privileged I am that you and others choose to spend some of it with me... or at least in the company of my writing.

I could go on, but I won't. Thanks again for reading and I hope you and my words will meet again soon.

Fandabulous bonus

Damn, I sound like an online marketing guru! Disregarding that... if you'd like to see some photos from our Smugglers days, featuring Joy and myself, *and* be informed when more writing and my next book comes out, simply copy and paste the following link into your web browser, and Bob's your Aunty...

http://eepurl.com/G947X

About the Author

Joe Cawley is a full-time writer, now living in the hills of Tenerife with his family and an assortment of other wildlife. He's the author of *More Ketchup than Salsa*, *Even More Ketchup than Salsa* and the co-author of *Moving to Tenerife*, a useful guide for those determined souls who haven't entirely been put off living in Tenerife after reading this and his other titles. When not writing, he's often found talking to his chickens, guinea pigs, turtles and fish.

Find out more about Joe and his other books at **www.joecawley.co.uk**.

Joe would be mighty pleased if you joined him and said hello on the following social media channels:

Twitter - @theWorldofJoe
Facebook - Facebook.com/JoeCawley

If you'd like to get in touch, please send a message to **writer@joecawley.co.uk** with any comments, opinions, requests or general waffle. Writing can be a lonely chore and any contact with the real world is greatly appreciated.

Made in the USA
Middletown, DE
30 May 2018